Conversations with Benjamin

Conversations with Benjamin

— *A Spirituality of Preaching that Heals* —

Martha Brune Rapp

RESOURCE *Publications* • Eugene, Oregon

CONVERSATIONS WITH BENJAMIN
A Spirituality of Preaching that Heals

Copyright © 2021 Martha Brune Rapp. All rights reserved. Except for brief quotations in critical publications or reviews, no part of this book may be reproduced in any manner without prior written permission from the publisher. Write: Permissions, Wipf and Stock Publishers, 199 W. 8th Ave., Suite 3, Eugene, OR 97401.

Resource Publications
An Imprint of Wipf and Stock Publishers
199 W. 8th Ave., Suite 3
Eugene, OR 97401

www.wipfandstock.com

PAPERBACK ISBN: 978-1-7252-9609-1
HARDCOVER ISBN: 978-1-7252-9608-4
EBOOK ISBN: 978-1-7252-9610-7

03/25/21

To Jim and all who heal,
even by their preaching.

Contents

List of Illustrations | ix
Preface | xi

Chapter 1: Encounter | 1

Chapter 2: The Aim of Preaching | 14

   Interlude: Reflection on the Collaborative Nature of God's Creation | 23

Chapter 3: Four Pylons of a Spirituality of Preaching that Heals | 24

   Interlude: Reflection on the Importance of Knowing How Things Are Put Together | 36

Chapter 4: Human Anthropology: The 'Anatomy' of Preaching that Heals | 38

Chapter 5: Pylon One: Gospel: Lessons for Preaching that Heals | 53

Chapter 6: Pylon Two: 'Intentional': A Path to Interiority for Preaching that Heals | 73

   Interlude: Reflection on Creation's Interrelatedness | 88

Chapter 7: Pylon Three: 'Holographic': The Vision and Science of Preaching that Heals | 90

   Interlude: Reflection on the Anxiety of Feeling Like Something Is Missing | 101

CONTENTS

Chapter 8: Pylon Four: 'Spoken': Communication Principles for Preaching that Heals | 102

Interlude: Reflection on Wellbeing | 117

Chapter 9: Retrospective | 118

Bibliography | 121

Illustrations

Figure 1: The Wondrous Human: The 'Anatomy' of Spiritual Transformation | 41

Figure 2: The Healthy Human: Clinebell's Seven Dimensions of Wellbeing | 50

Figure 3: Interiority Analysis: A Method for Self-Appropriation | 83

Figure 4: The Trajectory of Healing | 98

Figure 5: (untitled: simple communication model) | 104

Figure 6: (untitled: the intersection of communication) | 105

Figure 7: (untitled: communication model with interference) | 106

Preface

The LORD God formed man out of the clay of the ground
and blew into his nostrils the breath of life,
and so that man became a living being.

—Genesis 2:7

On Feb. 20, 2018, the day I wrote the last word of my doctoral thesis, I had a keen sense that the project into which I had poured myself was a lifeless mound of clay.

It mattered little that it represented nearly three years of intensive research, a lifetime of communication experience, dozens of interviews with a wide cross-section of Christian preachers, and endless prayer and contemplation. It mattered little that it had tested the last nerve of my incredible husband Jim, my thesis adviser Rev. Dr. Greg Heille, OP, or my thesis reader Rev. Dr. Kay Northcutt. As a communicator who had a world-class career in journalism, public relations, and corporate marketing before an infused-by-light conversion experience and call to ministry changed the direction of my life, I knew an important truth: *no communication is of value unless it is received.*

This truth haunted me: *What,* I wondered, *would it take to turn a 257-page research project (with appendices) that offers a vision, a path and a plan for preaching that heals into an accessible resource for preachers and preaching students?*

PREFACE

* * * *

The answer didn't come quickly or easily. In fact, it was a full year after I received my doctor of ministry degree in preaching from the Aquinas Institute of Theology before I felt a strong spiritual nudge to begin. Slowly I began dissecting my thesis, discerning content that mattered and content that could be trashed, and developing new outlines.

Throughout the process, I continued to talk with practicing preachers about their experiences and the type of resources they found helpful in their ministries. I also drew on my own experience. (I am a certified spiritual director and a chaplain who has served as president of a 90-member interdenominational volunteer group of clergy and lay ministers who provide 24/7 chaplaincy services for a 300-bed community hospital. Additionally, I facilitate spirituality awareness groups for persons hospitalized in adult behavioral medicine and child and adolescent units.) Most of all, I prayed for insight: *if I were meant to undertake this work, what form would it need to take?*

* * * *

When the answer about form finally came, it jolted me: *write a novella based on conversations between a young preacher and a spiritual guide.* Essentially, tell a story!

I had often used a story format for retreats and preaching, and the idea of repurposing a clearly-academic work with nearly three hundred footnotes, a bibliography of more than one hundred fifty entries, and dozens of flow charts and drawings was intriguing.

Deciding to test the idea, I sat down at my computer and began to write. Words flowed effortlessly and easily. "Benjamin" (named for my oldest grandson and frequent hiking partner with whom I have amazingly life-giving conversations) took on a life of his own. His character is a composite of many preachers—gifted and graced men and women, ordained and lay, from many denominations—who have shared their stories with me. Likewise,

PREFACE

"Sophia" is a synthesis of the many spiritual directors in my life. The setting is our family's tree farm, complete with hiking paths, fishing ponds, scenic overlooks, and—at this particular moment in time—even a partially-constructed bridge.

* * * *

But what about footnotes? As I was reminded in this writing process, novellas normally do not include them, and therein lies the rub:

Format aside, *Conversations with Benjamin: A Spirituality of Preaching that Heals* is a serious academic work. It uses Socratic dialogue to bring together resources from many fields and subjects—listed alphabetically, Cosmology, Pope Francis, Methodology, Preaching, Healing in the Gospels, and Spirituality of Healing.

Given the nature of this work, I decided after much consternation that footnotes were necessary and have chosen to include them.

* * * *

Finally—and with deep gratitude, I wish to thank the many people who have helped God to breathe life into my otherwise-lifeless mound of clay: my husband Jim; Rev. Dan Bergbower, a friend who opened the door to my ministry; Rev. Dr. Harry Byrne, OP, Marian Love, and Carla Mae Streeter, OP, whose formation in Aquinas Institute of Theology's Spiritual Direction program changed my life; my Spiritual Direction Supervision "sisters": Marian Love, Mary Beth Osiecki, Toni Petersen, Rev. Gayle Pope, and Terri Quillen; Anita Cleary, OP, a spiritual director whose wisdom has helped me to navigate some very challenging waters; Rev. Dan Brothers, who shepherded me through four units of Clinical Pastoral Education with good humor and grace; the faculty of Aquinas Institute of Theology's DMin program, especially Rev. Dr. Greg Heille, OP, Dr. Honora Werner, OP, Dr. Mary Margaret Pazdan, OP, and the

PREFACE

late Rev. Dr. Dan Harris, CM; Rev. Dr. Kay Northcutt, an amma in every sense of the word; the clergy, lay ministers, and chaplains with whom I serve; the Lilly Foundation, sponsor of the Aquinas Institute Delaplane Preaching Scholars initiative, and my esteemed cohort members, especially small-group mentors Rev. Dr. Heidi Johnson and Dr. Deborah Wilhelm.

Martha Brune Rapp, DMin

Aquinas Institute Delaplane Preaching Scholar
November 2020, Quincy, Illinois

— Chapter 1 —

Encounter

I.

Benjamin had expected to feel welcome relief as the hatchback of his well-traveled, shadow-black Kia Soul latched shut with a resounding click. Yet, as he slid into the driver's seat, started the engine, and backed out of the rectory garage, he realized his only sensation was dread.

He couldn't help contrasting the start of *this* vacation to past vacations. *Past* vacations had been eagerly anticipated breaks from class or the precious days between a summer job and the new school year. *Then,* he had always been enthralled by the prospect of new adventures and unstructured time with friends. He especially cherished his memories of the ten euphoric days after ordination to the priesthood nearly fifteen months ago. *Then,* everything seemed possible.

Somehow in the intervening months, graced euphoria had been displaced by the heavy weight of the call he had accepted. The reality of ministry had hit him with a vengeance. As he pulled on the interstate just outside of town, he wondered when it began. Was it the first time he'd had to celebrate Mass with a fever and a cough? The emergency call to the hospital in the middle of the night to be with a young couple whose two-month-old son had just died inexplicably? One too many perfunctory parish meetings? Mediating family fights and sometimes even fights between parishioners and parish groups? Descending into the depths of human loneliness during pastoral visits to the homebound?

These jolting experiences had given Benjamin a taste of priesthood that was a far cry from the pleasant semester-long parish internship during his last year in the seminary. *Now*—and even with the unwavering support of the pastor at the parish where he served as parochial vicar, Benjamin felt like a lost sheep who had no access to an earthly shepherd of his own.

Still more disturbingly, Benjamin knew that his biggest struggle had nothing to do with the personal, pastoral, or administrative challenges of priesthood. The cause of his growing anxiety was preaching.

* * * *

It wasn't that Benjamin had slept through his seminary preaching classes. If anything, he had been especially attentive, aware that his *own* vocation had been seeded by the talks he heard at a Teens Encounter Christ (TEC) retreat. They had changed his life.

Benjamin remembered attending TEC as a skeptical 16-year-old. Although he had arrived feeling like a loner far outside of the reach of his church, he left with an overwhelming sense of love, acceptance, and belonging. After careful discernment, Benjamin had come to believe he was called to help others find the same connection to God, each other, and the rest of creation through the priesthood. Preaching, he reasoned, was the key: unless people grasped the love of God, they could hardly be expected to respond to it through the sacraments and in the world.

Fortunately, the Roman Catholic Church agreed. As far back as 1982 the U.S. bishops affirmed that preaching was a priest's primary duty. The sentiment was more than echoed by Pope Francis, a preacher-pope who was passionate about preaching. And this focus on preaching wasn't just a Catholic thing. Benjamin's friends who pastored other denominations said that preaching was *their* most important responsibility as well.

As he drove past rolling fields of corn and soybeans, Benjamin wondered how his preaching had gone so terribly wrong. He'd *tried* to follow the process he had been taught in the seminary:

start early in the week . . . contemplate scriptures for the coming Sunday, noting any ideas that seem to jump out from the passages . . . turn to commentaries and other resources in the middle of the week after initial ideas have a chance to gel . . . pay special attention to any difficulties or challenges that emerge from text and reflection . . . and finally, prepare, revise, practice, and preach the homily. He thought he understood his congregation, and, on a couple of occasions, had even invited parishioners to participate in a homily preparation group.

Yet the harder Benjamin tried, the more impossible it all seemed. He was convinced his preaching was on a downward spiral—that it had no more impact that a hollow gong, and maybe less. At least the hollow gong wasn't alienating a congregation.

* * * *

Noticing that the sky was darkening as he drove west on this particularly muggy summer afternoon, Benjamin remembered preaching at his first Mass the Sunday after ordination. *Then*, everything was colored with promise. Family and friends who filled the sun-lit church leaned into his every word, and Benjamin experienced being lifted up by their energy and love.

Now he almost regretted this memory. It had given him a taste of being in communion with the people in the pews through preaching. The contrast between *then* and *now* was more than he could bear. He felt like his heart was breaking.

Driving into growing rumbles of thunder, Benjamin flailed out at God: "Why is this happening to me? Can't you make it stop?"

A fat raindrop splatted on his windshield, then another, then another and another, giving way to a torrential downpour. Slowing his speed to avoid hydroplaning on the rain-slick asphalt, Benjamin realized his cheeks were damp. Were they tears of fear? Of frustration? He suspected they were caused by something far worse: shame.

After years of believing that a minister's ability to preach was a reflection of his or her relationship with God, Benjamin was deeply ashamed. Worse, he was convinced that his lack of connection to God must be on display every time he stood at the ambo. At his wits' end, he uttered a bargaining plea: "Okay, God: if you want me to preach, show me what I'm missing," he prayed.

* * * *

The rain slowed to a steady but unrelenting shower as Benjamin turned down the gravel road that led to his family's farm. He unchained the front gate and drove around to the side entrance of the unoccupied, century-old, four-square farmhouse that had been updated to serve as a family get-away.

When Benjamin confided to his parents how much he needed a break, his parents suggested that he spend his vacation recharging at the farm. They even volunteered to stock the kitchen so he wouldn't have to bother. Benjamin gratefully accepted their offer.

Unlocking the farmhouse and dropping his duffel bag just inside the door, Benjamin acknowledged how exhausted he was. Without unpacking, he headed to the kitchen, uncapped a bottle of beer, and plopped down on the futon-couch in the blind-darkened front room. Lulled by the rhythmic sound of rain striking the metal roof, he quickly fell into a deep, enveloping sleep.

II.

Benjamin awoke, momentarily startled and disoriented as he tried to remember where he was. It was morning. He opened the blinds behind the futon where he had spent the night. Yesterday's rain had coated the brick-paved patio just outside with dewy radiance, and a foggy mist arose like incense off of a nearby soybean field on the other side of a windbreak of pine trees.

Realizing he had not eaten since leaving the rectory a day earlier, Benjamin carried his half-drank beer into the kitchen in search of more substantial sustenance. He measured Folger's into the ancient Mr. Coffee, grateful that his parents had stocked the kitchen. As he scrambled eggs and put bread in the toaster, he realized he felt more rested than he had in months.

In the light of day and the breath of prayer, Benjamin experienced a surge of hope. Yesterday's sultry, soul-weighing heaviness had given way to a sense that everything was new and possible. This sense had always been a special gift of the farm.

* * * *

Boundaries for the farm had been plotted more than two centuries earlier when the federal government established 160-acre land grants to attract settlers to the Midwest. Benjamin's grandfather had purchased roughly 120 acres of one such plot nearly seventy years earlier with a dream of turning part of the land into a nature preserve and a family retreat for future generations.

Benjamin could not remember a time when he had not known and loved the farm. There had been too many family reunions to recall . . . too many Saturday nights when he had bunked in the farmhouse with his grandparents, munching popcorn in front of *Saturday Night Live* and learning to play bridge . . . driving lessons over dirt paths through fresh-plowed fields before his legs were long enough to reach the pedals of the old yellow pickup truck . . . hikes along the bank of a creek that flowed through the pine forest in search of arrowheads and geodes.

Although the farm had fallen into serious disrepair in the years before his grandfather's death, Benjamin's father had been working to restore it to its previous promise. In the past ten years, his father had updated the farmhouse, resuscitated two ponds and stocked them with fish, cut more than four miles of hiking paths through the dense woods that covered a third of the land, and placed old stone-based bus-stop benches at especially scenic overlooks that dotted the land. Deer and wild turkeys flourished, and industrious otters built occasional dams in the creek. Best of all, family members had started to return for reunions and recreation.

Placing his breakfast dishes in the sink, Benjamin filled a water bottle and headed outside.

* * * *

He knew exactly where he was going: to a bridge that was being built over a recently re-excavated pond.

It seemed tragic to Benjamin that ponds could die, but he had witnessed such a death himself. During his grandfather's lengthy incapacitation, the pond in the wooded area closest to the farmhouse was suffocated by moss that depleted its oxygen and sucked the life out of all but a few hearty mud turtles. The once-vibrant fishing spot had begun to loom large as a painful testimony to dreams that were perishing with the dreamer.

In one of his more ambitious farm restoration projects, Benjamin's father had arranged to have the oxygen-starved pond drained and re-dug a couple years earlier. The new pond was expanded and now formed a large letter "C" with a wild-flower-carpeted peninsula protruding from its far side to the center. Before the rain and melting snow had a chance to refill the pond, massive telephone poles had been sunk vertically into the hard clay ground to serve as pylons for an eventual bridge to the peninsula. Now—*finally*—the actual bridge was under construction. Benjamin could hardly wait to see the progress.

As he neared the path leading to the new pond, Benjamin stopped short. For the second time that morning, he was startled and disoriented, fixated as a figure emerged from the woods and walked toward him.

He felt himself freeze as a woman approached and said, "I've been expecting you."

III.

Failing to disguise his fear, Benjamin demanded, "Who *are* you? What are you doing here? This is private property. You shouldn't even *be* here, let alone claiming to be expecting me!"

Sidetracking his questions, the mysterious woman replied, "I can understand your fear and irritation. You came here to find tranquility, and I am intruding. But clearly, you can see that I am not here to harm you . . ."

Benjamin pushed back, "That's not the point. This is private property, and you are trespassing."

The intruder nodded, "Yes, of course, you are correct. I have entered your space and caught you off guard." Pausing, she added, "Whether I stay or go is entirely up to you. I will leave any time you say. But let me tell you one thing before you decide: I have been sent here to help you."

* * * *

"Help *me*?" Benjamin exclaimed incredulously. "You don't even *know* me! How can you possibly *help* me?"

"Actually, I *do* know you," the woman said softly. "I've always been present in your life."

"If that's *true*—and I'm not calling you a liar—I certainly don't *remember* you," Benjamin objected.

"Probably not," she agreed. "But whether you recognize me from your past hardly matters. I've been sent to help you *now*."

"Not to be rude, but how can you possibly help me? What do you even *know* about me?" Benjamin repeated.

Looking tenderly at him, the woman replied softly, "I know you are suffering. I know you have chosen to spend your vacation *here* because you are struggling to make sense out of something important and troubling in your life. And I know that people who love you and care about you recognize that you are in pain and are praying you will find a resolution."

Feeling taken aback, Benjamin insisted, "Who told you this?"

"Again, why does this matter?" the woman asked. "*Many* people care. Isn't it enough to know that those who love you sense you are in trouble and are praying for you? That through their prayers, I've been sent to offer you help?"

Despite himself, Benjamin asked with curiosity, "So . . . just what kind of help do *they*, whoever *they* are, think I need?"

"That's just it," the woman replied. "They haven't a clue. You really haven't told them anything directly, but as you well know, we can tell when those we love are hurting. Although you've tried to keep it to yourself, you've communicated your pain through the flatness in your voice . . . your body language . . . the energy you exude . . . in so many ways!"

Pausing, she continued, "There are other signs as well. For one, you've always vacationed with friends who share your love of hiking and adventure. But not this year. You've become withdrawn and tense—like a different person."

Letting go of his last vestige of bravado, Benjamin admitted in a near-whisper, "You are right."

* * * *

Gently the woman suggested, "Why don't we walk to the new bridge and talk, Benjamin. Isn't that where you were heading before I interrupted?"

"Yes, that's where I was heading, and I probably *do* need to talk," he conceded. "But first, tell me: how do you know my name?"

"I've *always* known it," the woman replied. "Benjamin is one of my favorite names—the ancient Hebrew name that means 'son of the right hand.'"

After a moment, Benjamin ventured, "If I'm going to bare my soul to you, won't you at least tell me *your* name?"

"Of course," the woman answered. "It's Sophia."

"Wisdom," Benjamin whispered.

IV.

Benjamin and Sophia entered the cool forest where the bridge was under construction. A path wide enough for hikers and even farm vehicles had been built up, separating a shallow wooded gulley on the left from the freshly-dug pond on the right.

As ponds go, this one was massive, covering nearly two acres. Benjamin was surprised to see blue-green water lapping its banks.

ENCOUNTER

Had it really already been almost three years since he and his father stood at this very place staring at the pond's lowest point, which then boasted two or three inches of accumulated water after the first post-excavation rainstorm? Benjamin had wondered whether the pond would ever be filled.

The bridge stood proudly just past the pond's halfway point. Piles of lumber on the path attested to work still to be done.

As they approached, Benjamin could see the twelve-foot-wide bridge that now extended from pathway to peninsula. Side rails still needed to be built and—much to Benjamin's amusement—two steps to the bridge were under construction on the path side to prevent more rambunctious family members from driving the recreational vehicle, a Polaris Ranger, across the expanse and ending up in the water.

What surprised Benjamin the most were two Adirondack chairs angled toward each other at the center of the bridge.

"Would you like to sit?" Sophia invited.

Benjamin nodded, "Yes."

* * * *

Benjamin and Sophia sat quietly for a while. They felt no immediate need to talk. It was as if the *wrong* words (that is, *gratuitous* words spoken merely to fill the silence) would desecrate this sacred space.

The pond was mesmerizing. Benjamin spent many minutes watching concentric ripples emerge from the water and take on lives of their own before expanding into nothingness . . . tracking minuscule air bubbles that traced underwater life . . . and watching wind-shifting reflections of trees and prairie grass on the pond's surface. From the vantage point of the bridge, the pond looked entirely different than it had from the path.

Sophia noticed the difference too. Eventually, she broke the silence: "What we see truly *does* depend on where we stand—or in our case, *sit*," she reflected. "It changes our perspective."

As her words faded into the air, she turned to Benjamin and gently asked, "Are you ready to begin?"

* * * *

That night as Benjamin reflected on his morning encounter, he realized his perspective on preaching *had* changed. Under Sophia's gentle questioning, he had begun to see the path that brought him to this point—to this encounter—in a far different light.

When Benjamin told Sophia that he had become convinced God did not want him to preach, Sophia had gently asked, "What if God not only *wants* you to preach but is calling you to become a great preacher? What if you are being invited to develop a gift?"

Benjamin was sure his surprise had registered on his face.

Sophia continued, "Great discomfort *can* be an indication that the Holy Spirit is prodding us to go deeper and to discover more—not just for our own good, but for the good of those we serve."

As Benjamin pondered this idea, Sophia pressed on. "Tell me about your preaching classes," she urged.

"I had two—six semester hours in total," he replied. "They were part of the Master of Divinity curriculum that every seminarian was required to complete."

"What did your preaching classes cover?" Sophia asked.

After thinking for a moment, Benjamin replied, "We learned a process for preparing homilies and sermons—contemplate the Scripture passages to be preached, study them, write and practice the homily or sermon, then preach it. We practiced preparing different kinds of sermons, and sometimes we preached them in class."

A funny look crossed Benjamin's face. "Come to think of it, we actually *wrote* more sermons than we ever *preached*," he reflected.

"And what about classes in Scripture?" Sophia prodded.

"Two overview classes were required: one on Old Testament and one on New," he replied. "We could take electives in Scripture if our schedules permitted, but the schedule was packed!"

"What about the rest of the program?" Sophia asked.

"It was grueling," Benjamin admitted. "We—both seminarians and lay students in the Master of Divinity program—were required to complete nearly one-hundred credit hours in an enormous variety of subjects. Philosophy of theology. Two classes in the history of Christianity. Ecclesiology. Christology. Morality. Pastoral counseling. Liturgy. Sacraments. Catechesis. A semester of field practice. And—for seminarians, presiding—*in addition to* Biblical studies and preaching."

He continued, "Seminarians also had ongoing spiritual formation, which largely focused on prayer, discernment, and our individual calls to the priesthood."

Sophia looked at Benjamin with compassion.

"Then I got ordained and was assigned to a parish," Benjamin continued. "It didn't take me long to realize I was in over my head. Preaching was the culprit . . . a constant barrage of homilies—Sunday, daily Masses, funerals, weddings—on top of everything else.

"So much for the preaching process; it's kind of gone up in smoke," he confessed, "and I am exhausted—overwhelmed. The truth is, I feel like I'm failing."

"I think you are being too hard on yourself," Sophia softly replied.

* * * *

As they talked, Benjamin had to admit Sophia had a point. The seminary had been like drinking out of a firehose. Before you could quench your thirst from one hose, you were being doused by another.

"The seminary gave you a strong foundation," Sophia affirmed, "with an enormous variety of tools, techniques, and disciplines that are already playing a vital role in your ministry and will continue to do so. But something important seems to be missing."

"What is that?" Benjamin asked.

"An integrating spirituality of preaching," Sophia replied.

V.

"An integrating spirituality of preaching . . . ?" Benjamin puzzled.

"Let's break this down," Sophia responded. "The integrating spirituality I am proposing is a *conscious, overarching,* and *intentional* life orientation. It is *conscious* because we are aware of it. It is *overarching* because it umbrellas every part of our lives, providing meaning, value, and cohesion. It is *intentional* because it is a deliberate choice to *be* a certain way in the world. It guides how we think and choose."

She paused, waiting for Benjamin to absorb her words.

"And preaching—how does *that* fit in?" Benjamin asked.

"Preaching is how we give voice to this spirituality, with or without words," Sophia replied.

"We preach—that is, we give voice to our spirituality—through our very presence in the world: through our body language, the words we speak, our tone of voice, our facial expressions, the things we do and the way we do them," she continued. "It is far more than Sunday preaching at the pulpit. It is the compassion we offer to parishioners in the hospital on Monday . . . the way we treat the cashier at the supermarket on Tuesday . . . the high-fives we exchange with school children . . . our patience at parish meetings . . . how we answer the phone or greet people who interrupt us. *All* of these forms of preaching flow from our spirituality . . . our *conscious, overarching,* and *intentional* life orientation."

* * * *

After several minutes, Benjamin observed, "This is different than how I've been approaching ministry."

"Can you say more about this?" Sophia invited.

"In the past, I've thought of everything I do as a compartmentalized task," Benjamin said. "I've tended to see the tools, techniques, and disciplines from seminary more as ends in themselves. But with an overarching spirituality of preaching, they become integrated parts of a cohesive *whole.* Everything flows from this whole."

Sophia nodded.

"Now, let's consider the *Christian* spirituality of preaching," she continued. "*This* conscious, overarching, and intentional life orientation is centered on love. Jesus Christ is the preached Word of God (Who Is Love) in the world. Christ continues to be made known through the Holy Spirit—that is, a graced *consciousness of the whole*. A Christian spirituality of preaching aims to communicate this truth in a way that attracts others to ever-greater justice, wholeness and goodness—to ever-greater communion enabled by love."

Inspired, Benjamin affirmed, "Transforming love communicated *by* and *through* the Inspirited Word . . ."

"Yes," Sophia smiled. "Inspirited Word (of Love) Made Flesh so it may dwell among us."

* * * *

"Earlier, you told me how crucial the Teens Encounter Christ weekend you attended was in your life," Sophia had said. "You said you left TEC with an overwhelming sense of love, acceptance, and belonging—that you wanted others to find what you had found. Your TEC experience led you to a relationship with God and life in the Spirit, mediated by Jesus Christ. It also informed your decision to become a priest."

Pausing, she added, "Do you see how this vision could meld with a spirituality of preaching?"

"Yes," Benjamin said, "but I suspect there is so much more to it!"

"There *is*," Sophia agreed, "but as Jesus would say, you cannot hear it now. You need quiet time to process everything we have already discussed." Continuing, she volunteered, "If you would like, I am willing to spend time with you each day while you are at the farm. We can work together . . ."

Benjamin replied, "I would like that."

Before they took leave, Benjamin and Sophia agreed to meet on the bridge the next morning to consider the aim of preaching.

— Chapter 2 —

The Aim of Preaching

I.

Benjamin was not surprised to see that Sophia was already at the bridge when he arrived for their meeting early the next morning.

"How *are* you today?" she asked warmly.

"I think I'm relieved," Benjamin said.

"Relieved?" Sophia questioned. "An interesting word . . ."

"Relieved," Benjamin repeated. "When I decided to forego my typical vacation and come to the farm instead, I felt the need to come to terms with preaching. But I wasn't sure *how*. Although I'd planned to pray about it and re-read books from my preaching classes, I didn't have a clear focus for the week. But as we talked yesterday, my perspective changed."

"Can you put the change into words?" Sophia pressed.

"I think I *can*," Benjamin said. "Let me try."

After several moments, he continued: "I see now that ordination was the *beginning* of ministry more than the end of prescribed education and formation. I see that the Master of Divinity program merely *introduced* tools, information, processes, and disciplines needed to help guide the church, but it didn't make me proficient. I also see that the Holy Spirit is *continuing* to work in my life—that even disappointments and frustrations can be proddings to move forward. Spiritual formation is an ongoing, lifelong process."

Sophia nodded encouragingly.

"I also see that ministry needs to be more than an ongoing succession of fragmented tasks," he continued. "It really *does* need to flow from a *conscious, overarching,* and *intentional* spirituality—a life orientation that centers on preaching."

"And how would you define preaching *now*?" Sophia prodded.

"As the act of expressing God's love in everything we do or say," Benjamin said. "Love is the most attractive force in the world. It draws people to God."

"You *are* a good student," Sophia smiled.

* * * *

"Today, we are going to go deeper," she ventured. "Have you ever thought about the *aim* of preaching?"

Benjamin looked confused. "Isn't the aim of preaching obvious?" he asked.

"Maybe not as obvious as we'd like to think," Sophia replied. "Let me ask you this: what are some of the ways other ministers might respond when asked about the *aim* of preaching?"

Benjamin thought for a minute. "Well, they *might* say that the aim of preaching is to teach a congregation more about Scripture. As Saint Jerome said, ignorance of Scripture is ignorance of Christ," he began.

"Yes, knowing Scripture is important," Sophia affirmed. "Go on . . ."

"Well, they *might* say that we preach to get people to repent—to keep them from going to hell. Or that we preach to get people to be obedient to God just as Jesus was obedient unto death on the cross," he continued. "Or they *might* say we preach to teach doctrine and to catechize—to explain what our denomination teaches and why."

"You've easily named four very different focuses: Bible, repentance, obedience, and catechesis," Sophia summarized. "But do any of these resonate with you as preaching's overall aim?"

"Not really, even though they are all important," Benjamin replied.

"I agree," Sophia concurred. "So, what do *you* think the aim of preaching is?"

"It is more," Benjamin replied, "but I can't find the word I am looking for."

"Pope Francis *has* found the word," Sophia said, "and that word is healing."

II.

Benjamin quietly pondered what Sophia had said. He knew that Pope Francis was a member of the Society of Jesus, a religious order commonly known as the Jesuits. As a Jesuit, the pope had been formed in Ignatian spirituality,[1] a concrete and practical way of life that seeks to bring God's healing love to the world. This spirituality sees God as a loving giver of gifts who deals personally with each human being and is everywhere, active, and working in our world.

However, Ignatian spirituality also recognizes that the world is seriously broken with illness, blindness, diminishment, and poverty of all types. Benjamin knew that human beings, who are created to know, love, and serve God, can participate in what Jesuit Brian Grogan calls the "divine project to win the world with love"—*if* they are free to do so.

He also knew that healing aims to undo the captivity of greed, hatred, and disordered affections that control people and limit their freedom to choose. It is enabled by a commitment to put God at the center of all decision-making and to live as "contemplatives in action" who seek to discern and follow the will of God (which is always the greatest good) in every situation.

Finally, as if reading Benjamin's mind, Sophia broke the silence: "Pope Francis embodies a spirituality of preaching that heals, and he challenges us to do the same."

---

1. Information on Jesuit spirituality is based on Grogan, "Ignatian Way #2."

THE AIM OF PREACHING

* * * *

"I understand the *concept*, but I'm not sure how to act on it," Benjamin admitted.

"Would it be helpful to see how Pope Francis applied this spirituality to one of the most difficult situations imaginable—his election as pope?" Sophia asked.

"It would be," Benjamin assented.

"Then let me tell you the story," Sophia offered. "Feel free to interrupt with thoughts or questions." After a pause, she began:

"Jorge Bergoglio adopted a spirituality of preaching that heals years before he became pope. His spirituality was honed during painful times of trial and error as a young priest in Argentina, tested through a long vocation of prayerful examen and reflection, and remarkably lived when he was Archbishop of Buenos Aires. But it wasn't until he became the 266th pope of the Roman Catholic Church on March 13, 2013 that he captured the world's imagination. From his first appearance as pope, he *exuded* healing.

"The Roman Catholic Church was in the throes of what German theologian Hans Küng describes as its 'deepest crisis in confidence since the Reformation'[2] nearly five centuries earlier. Much of the crisis was caused by the church's own actions: highly publicized financial scandals, mishandling of clergy sexual abuse charges, mistreatment of women and other groups,[3] internal attempts to reverse the direction of the Second Vatican Council,[4] and a heavy-handed and alienating magisterium[5]—but there was more.

"The Catholic Church (along with *every* established denomination in the Western World) was facing what Erskine Clarke described as 'the disappearance of the social function the churches once fulfilled.'[6] Western culture no longer regarded Christianity as the judge and authority on matters of morality (or much of

---

2. Küng, *Can We Save the Catholic Church?*, 12.
3. Boff, *Francis of Assisi, Francis of Rome*, 9.
4. Küng, *Can We Save the Catholic Church?*, 12–13.
5. Mannion, *Pope Francis*, lecture six.
6. Brueggemann et al., *Exilic Preaching*, 1.

anything else). As Dominican theologian-preacher Carla Mae Streeter observed, there was a tendency to relegate all religions to the realm of myths for the childish.[7]

"The Catholic Church tried to regain its position with approaches that had served it well in the past. For example, Küng cited the bedazzling 'return of Baroque splendor and impressively staged papal liturgies used by Rome to demonstrate the presence of a strong church and the pope [and] papal youth rallies, attended for the most part by conservative, charismatic youth groups and promoted by traditionalist organizations.'[8] And Gerald Mannion cited 'doctrinal clampdowns alongside the prevalence of authoritarianism and imposed uniformity across the church.'[9] However, these efforts seemed to do more harm than good," Sophia concluded.

Benjamin recalled, "I was in the seminary in college philosophy at the time, and I felt like I had to defend my vocation to the priesthood to others all of the time."

"It must have been painful," Sophia said. "Devoted and blameless priests, seminarians, and religious men and women throughout our country found themselves under relentless attack, and many didn't have the strength to tough it out. When Pope Francis was elected in March 2013, the Roman Catholic Church was facing what Küng called 'a gradual withering away' with the loss of tens of thousands of priests and a decline in the number of people entering religious life.[10] In the United States alone, 15 percent of the population identified itself as 'former Catholics'[11] and Sunday Mass attendance had dwindled to 24 percent."[12]

"How would you even begin to deal with such a crisis?" Benjamin asked.

7. Streeter, *Foundations of Spirituality*, 4–5.
8. Küng, *Can We Save the Catholic Church?*, 19.
9. Mannion, *Pope Francis*, lecture six.
10. Küng, *Can We Save the Catholic Church?*, 17.
11. Jones and Cox, "The Francis Effect?," http://www.prri.org.
12. Pew Research Center, "'Strong' Catholic Identity at Four-Decade Low in U.S.," www.pewforum.org.

"And here's where our story picks up," Sophia said, "with what Dominican preacher-homiletician Gregory Heille calls the 'show me, don't tell me' quality of good preaching."[13]

* * * *

"For the first six months of his papacy, Pope Francis demonstrated a spirituality of preaching that heals mostly through his actions. He recognized the Church was in the grip of illness, stuck in an abyss of its own making, and that nothing short of deep healing would begin to turn the tide," Sophia said.

"The healing began from his first moments as pope when Pope Francis stepped out on the central balcony of Saint Peter Basilica to greet the 150-thousand people assembled below *without* the customary papal regalia. Then he asked the crowd to silently pray for him. The next day Pope Francis did something equally startling for a pope. He went to the guest house where he had stayed during the papal conclave and paid his bill," Sophia said.

Benjamin mused, "Christ-like acts—precisely what you might expect from the pope, and yet so noteworthy . . . "

"So noteworthy that just one week after Pope Francis's election, British Catholic journalist Austen Ivereigh wrote that the new pope was already causing a 'quiet earthquake' and a 'gentle revolution,'"[14] Sophia concurred.

"Everything Pope Francis did—his choice of name, refusing the expensive accouterments that had seeped into the papacy . . . choosing to live in a community rather than the papal apartments . . . visiting a prison and washing the feet of youth offenders, both male and female, Christian and Muslim, on the Holy Thursday just after his election . . . refusing to pass judgment on

---

13. Heille, *The Preaching of Pope Francis*, 2.

14. Ivereigh, "Pope Francis takes fresh approach to papacy," *OSV Newsweekly*, March 20, 2013, https://www.osv.com/OSVNewsweekly/Story?TabId/2672/ArtMID/13567/ArticleID/7879/Pope-Francis-takes-fresh-approach-to-papacy.aspx.

homosexuality—preached a message of healing more forcibly than words," Sophia said.

"But what is really important is that Pope Francis's words and actions were not calculated and staged. They flowed naturally in response to God's grace," Sophia continued. "It was the paradigm-changing impact of his graced energy that caused *millions* to become Francis watchers long before they understood it as healing.

"In fact, Pope Francis didn't even *use* the word 'healing' until the following September when he challenged *all* preachers to heal, *every time they preach*,"[15] she added.

III.

Benjamin spoke quietly, "Based on the pope's example, I'd say his challenge is huge."

"It *is*," Sophia agreed. "Certainly, it is rooted in Ignatian spirituality—ongoing, intentional discernment of God's will, which is always the greatest good. But there's more. Humility. The desire for a genuine encounter with others. Magnanimity (the opposite of small-mindedness). Inclusivity. Appreciation for the interrelatedness of All That Is. And mercy.

"His challenge really *is* to embrace a spirituality of preaching that heals," she added.

"I have a sense that this is from God," Benjamin mused.

Nodding, Sophia said, "It *is* from God. Through contemplation, Pope Francis saw that the Roman Catholic Church had turned in on itself, becoming more defensive and self-reverential than evangelistic and outward-looking. He saw that his beloved church had become so focused on reclaiming its past that it could not see the needs of the present that were right before its eyes."

---

15. Spadaro, "A Big Heart Open to God," *America Magazine*, September 30, 2013.

THE AIM OF PREACHING

* * * *

Benjamin reflected, "That's so true! It's hard to think of others when you are preoccupied with yourself—when you're afraid or feel you're being attacked."

"Exactly!" Sophia said. "Pope Francis knew he had to break the pattern of thought that had brought the church to its present position on a spiraling downward trajectory. That is why he suggested that the church thinks of itself in a new, *out*reaching, missionary way—*as a field hospital after battle.*

"As Pope Francis said, 'I see clearly that the thing the church needs most today is the ability to heal the wounds and to warm the hearts of the people. It is useless to ask a seriously ill person if he has high cholesterol or about the level of his blood sugars! You have to heal his wounds. Then we can talk about everything else.'"[16]

"But how do we know what those wounds are?" Benjamin asked.

"The people of God will tell us if we have the heart to meet them where they are and the grace to *really* listen," Sophia replied. "This is difficult because it requires that we suspend judgment and trust the healing love of God."

She continued, "The pope described our mission this way: 'The ministers of the Gospel must be people who can warm the hearts of the people, who walk through the dark night with them, who know how to dialogue and to descend themselves into their people's night, into their darkness, without getting lost. The people of God want pastors, not clergy acting like bureaucrats or government officials.'"[17]

* * * *

Again Benjamin grew quiet.
"Your thoughts?" Sophia encouraged.

---

16. Spadaro, *A Big Heart Open to God*, 24.
17. Spadaro, *A Big Heart Open to God*, 32.

"There has got to be a place for doctrine and for catechesis," Benjamin said. "Aren't there times when even *pastors* must rely on them?"

"Certainly," Sophia said emphatically. "Doctrine and catechesis are, and always will be, important. Pope Francis wasn't saying that preaching doesn't have to be doctrinally correct; however, he was recognizing that there is an intelligent order to the preaching and healing dynamic, and that order begins with the proclamation of God's saving love."

She continued, "As the pope said, 'A beautiful homily, a genuine sermon must begin with the first proclamation, the proclamation of salvation . . . Then you have to do catechesis. Then you can draw even a moral consequence. But the proclamation of the saving love of God comes before moral and religious imperatives.'[18]

"Essentially," Sophia concluded, "the spirituality of preaching that heals—the challenge of Pope Francis—is nothing less than a challenge to return to the preaching-healing paradigm in the Gospels and to follow Jesus's example through our Church, our field hospital for souls."

* * * *

Sophia glanced at Benjamin, who was staring at the pond, deep in thought.

"We've been talking for quite a while about some profound ideas," she said gently. "I think it is time for a break. What do you think?"

"So many ideas are swimming in my head: the aim of preaching. Preaching to heal. Preaching without words. The idea of the church as a field hospital after battle. Healing as a return to the Gospel," Benjamin said. "I could use some time to process everything, and I'd like to take a hike."

The two agreed to return to the bridge that evening to explore the characteristics of preaching that heals.

---

18. Spadaro, *A Big Heart Open to God*, 35.

— Interlude —

Reflection on the Collaborative Nature of God's Creation

As Benjamin hiked through the pine forest that afternoon, he felt more alive than he had for months. Certainly it did not hurt that it was an idyllic summer afternoon or that he was at one of his favorite places in the world, but there was more. He had a sense of hopefulness he'd thought was lost forever.

After holding on to a burden that had become heavier the longer he carried it, Benjamin had finally started to let go. He knew now that it was never his weight to carry alone—that God had created a collaborative world.

This very place, this farm, was collaborative: God's creation lovingly tended by human hands . . . land to be worked and revered . . . a place of initiative and a refuge of peace.

The very people in his life were collaborative: his pastor who was covering Benjamin's ministry this week . . . his grandparents who had envisioned the need for a place of re-creation . . . his father who was reviving the farm's vision and building a bridge . . . his mother who had stocked the kitchen . . . and now, Sophia. They were all people of grace, living more and more into love through a spirituality of preaching that heals. It was more than collaborative. It was connected; it was communion.

"I don't have to go it alone and I never did," Benjamin prayed aloud as he breathed in the pine-scented air. Infused by the presence of God Who Is Love, he was at peace.

— Chapter 3 —

Four Pylons of a Spirituality of Preaching that Heals

I.

Sophia greeted Benjamin warmly as he returned to the bridge that evening.

"How *are* you?" she asked.

"Lighter!" Benjamin exclaimed, describing his afternoon hike. "Even better than that, *connected!*"

"Connected," Sophia echoed. Benjamin noticed a smile flash across her face.

"I'm smiling because your new-found sense of connectedness indicates that you may be experiencing healing yourself," she explained.

"My favorite metaphor for healing is that it is a process of bridge-building," she continued. "A bridge connects Point A to Point B by spanning *something.*"

Benjamin looked at her quizzically. "But what does this healing bridge connect and what does it span?" he asked.

"*This* metaphoric bridge connects *head* and *heart*," Sophia replied. "The Sioux Indians have a saying that the longest distance is the eighteen inches between the human head and the heart. We can think of the head as the human spirit, the zero ground of a person's thinking and choosing, and the heart as God Who Is Love.

"The two are separated by a deep abyss that holds everything that keeps us from love of self, others, and God: *fear, selfishness, greed, disordered desires, prejudice*: the list is endless.

Bridge-building is the long and often-difficult process of reorienting our lives to God . . . that is, to love."

* * * *

"Is this why you suggested we begin our meetings on the bridge?" Benjamin asked.

"It is," Sophia said softly. "I especially like *this* bridge because it is still under construction. Although there are missing steps, siderails to be built, and finishing to be done, it is still recognizable as a bridge that connects path to peninsula."

"The bridge is recognizable *now*," Benjamin mused.

"Yes," Sophia agreed, "but you saw it before it was recognizable—when it was no more than evenly-spaced telephone poles, pylons as they are technically called. Pylons are the critical foundation that support most bridges."

Closing his eyes to envision the image, Benjamin finally said, "So, if we are building a bridge that connects *head* and *heart*, we should start with the pylons."

"Right," Sophia affirmed. "Our first step is to establish pylons that will support our bridge—in this case, characteristics of a spirituality of preaching that heals."

"I am ready," Benjamin said.

* * * *

"Would you mind terribly if I go into teaching mode, Benjamin?" Sophia asked. "We only have a little over an hour until sunset and there's a great deal to cover."

"I don't mind," he said, reaching into his backpack for a notebook and pen.

"Preaching that heals rests on four pylons," Sophia began. "It is easy to remember them with an acrostic: *G/IHS*."

Benjamin interjected, "I get the IHS—the Greek abbreviation of Jesus's name. But what about the G?"

"The _G_ospel of Jesus—G/IHS," Sophia replied. "*I* is for *i*n*tentional*; H, for _h_*olistic* (or, as Dominican preacher-healer Gregory Heille says, _h_*olographic*[1]); and S, for _s_*poken*."

II.

Sophia continued, "G, our first pylon, reminds us that the _G_ospel is at the center of everything we say and do. It is surprisingly easy to forget that our church exists for only one reason, to bring about the *basileia* of God through service to the Gospel, the Good News of Jesus, the Christ.

"As theologian Hans Küng so aptly observes, 'The crucial question is always the same: Does one's church faithfully incorporate and reflect the original Christian message, the Gospel, which to all intents and purposes is Jesus Christ himself, to whom each church appeals as its ultimate authority, or is it mainly a church system with a Christian label? . . . Without a concrete and consequent return to the historical Jesus, to his message, his behavior and his fate . . . a Christian church—whatever its name—will have neither the true Christian identity nor relevance for modern human beings and society.'"[2]

"That makes sense," Benjamin interjected. "*Of course* the Gospel must be at the center."

* * * *

"But there's more," Sophia said. "Preaching that heals responsibly appropriates the Gospel for our time and culture. It accommodates advances in human knowledge. As much as many would wish, we simply cannot deny or ignore breakthroughs in science, human anthropology, or other fields of study!

"There is no question that much of what we know today was unimaginable in Jesus's world or that human knowledge is

---

1. Heille, *The Preaching of Pope Francis*, 17.
2. Küng, *Can We Save the Catholic Church?*, 57–58.

FOUR PYLONS OF A SPIRITUALITY OF PREACHING THAT HEALS

expanding at an exponential rate. Our ability to understand what God has revealed continues to deepen because *this is how God designed creation!* To close our eyes to science is to deny God's very creation.

"Scientist-theologian Heidi Ann Russell includes a great quote from the late George V. Coyne, director emeritus of the Vatican Observatory, in her book *Quantum Shift: Theology and Pastoral Implications of Contemporary Developments in Science*: 'We do not need God to explain the universe as we see it today. But once I believe in God, the universe as I see it today says a great deal about the God in whom I believe.'"[3]

Benjamin summarized, "Then, our challenge is to be faithful to Scripture without ignoring advances in human knowledge, which, after all, God ordained through creation."

"Exactly," Sophia said.

* * * *

"Let's consider how appropriating the Gospel for our time might impact preaching," Sophia continued. "For example, since the beginning of the twentieth century we have learned through science how utterly interrelated God's creation is. As Pope Francis reflects, 'Time and space are not independent of one another, and not even atoms or subatomic particles can be considered in isolation.'"[4]

"Without much difficulty we can see how this scientific breakthrough deepens the meaning of the Gospel idea that whatever we do to the least of God's people or to any part of creation, we do to God," she said. "We no longer can imagine that we have the right to dominate creation in a way that destroys it and subjugates others."

"This is the pope's thinking in *Laudato Si'*, his encyclical on the need to care for our environment," Benjamin said.

Sophia nodded. "Interestingly though—and as Pope Francis himself stresses, within this interconnected world where each is

---

3. Russell, *Quantum Shift*, 104.
4. Francis, *Laudato Si'*, paragraph 138.

dependent on the other and all is a product of creative love, there is a new appreciation for the uniqueness of human beings.

"In *Laudato Si'*, Pope Francis writes that the human being is unique in ways that '... cannot be fully explained by the evolution of other open systems.' He writes, 'Each of us has his or her own personal identity and is capable of entering into dialogue with others and with God himself. Our capacity to reason, to develop arguments, to be inventive, to interpret reality and to create art, along with other not yet discovered capacities, are signs of uniqueness which transcends the spheres of biology.'"[5]

Benjamin reflected, "Scripture tells us that human beings are made in the image and likeness of God..."

"Yes," Sophia said, "and among the most important advances in our time is an understanding of what this means—just *how* unique the human spirit is. Essentially, when the *head* is connected to the *heart*—that is, when the human spirit is consciously aware of God Who Is Love in every thought, word and deed, we become capable of recognizing and responding to needs and injustices in the world. We become the graced conduits of God's healing love that God has created us to be," Sophia said.

"The hands and feet of Christ," Benjamin affirmed.

III.

"Our second pylon is *I* for *intentional*," Sophia said. "Preaching that heals is always intentional. It *aims* to heal—to build a bridge between *head* and *heart*.

"The intentionality we are talking about requires the personal discipline to live a life of ongoing discernment and prayer. It cooperates with grace, seeking the will of God (which, again, is always the greatest good) in every situation."

She paused, "Later this week we will talk about a method that can help a person be more intentional. For now, though, it is enough to know that preaching that heals normally does not just

---

5. Francis, *Laudato Si'*, paragraph 81.

happen on its own. It flows from an intentional, *on-purpose* life orientation—a spirituality."

* * * *

Benjamin protested, "But isn't *all* preaching intentional? The homilies I write and preach don't just happen. I *choose* to spend time on them."

"Of course all preaching has some degree of intentionality, but most preaching does not heal or—as disgruntled parishioners often complain—do much of anything else," Sophia said. "In fact (and not to offend you), a great deal of preaching (perhaps *most*!) merely reinforces long-held biases and clichés or paraphrases the readings the congregation just heard. It does absolutely nothing to strengthen the *head*-to-*heart* bridge in any meaningful way. It merely fills designated space in a liturgy."

"Ouch," Benjamin said.

"Ouch is right," Sophia agreed "Preaching that fails to heal—as homiletician Daniel Harris put it, *to fund a new imagination*[6]—is destructive. It drives people away from church and closes them off to the Gospel. When people say 'I'm not being fed,' they are saying that they are not being nourished with challenging words that fill them with hope and healing—words they can use to transform their lives and ultimately, the world."

Benjamin stopped writing and sat quietly.

"What are you thinking," Sophia said.

"I'm thinking about the difference it would make if I were to approach every part of preaching with the *intention* of identifying illness and offering healing," he said with excitement. "It would change how I read Scripture, how I think about the congregation, the stories I tell, the words I use—*everything*!"

"Do you think it would make preaching more difficult or easier?" Sophia asked.

"So much easier and so much better!" Benjamin exclaimed.

---

6. Harris, *We Speak the Word of the Lord*, 146–147.

IV.

"The third pylon is H for *holistic*, or better, *holographic vision*," Sophia continued. "Preaching that heals has a holistic or holographic understanding of illness."

"How do you define 'holistic' and 'holographic' in this context?" Benjamin asked.

"'Holistic' means that illness affects the whole. 'Holographic' goes much deeper, capturing the utter interrelatedness of God's creation where All is inextricably connected, continuously *influencing* and *being influenced* by the other," Sophia said.

"When we say that preaching that heals is *holographic*, we are acknowledging that it recognizes creation's interrelatedness. *No illness exists in isolation*," she stressed. "*Every* illness is communal, arising from depletion of the human spirit caused by evil in the world. Depletion of the smallest or the seemingly most insignificant among us affects every dimension of human existence, up to the very cosmos in which we live.

"Jesus demonstrated that human beings can be diminished in two ways: by being afflicted or by participating in a system that causes, perpetuates, and/or tolerates *any* sickness of the other, whether intentionally or inadvertently, voluntarily or involuntarily. Jesus healed both forms of diminishment, restoring the afflicted person to a state of health and challenging conditions that enabled the affliction in the first place," Sophia concluded.

* * * *

"Our culture does not understand illness *or* healing this way," Benjamin observed.

"You bring up an important point," Sophia agreed. "Contemporary Western culture tends to look at healing in a very narrow way. Our understanding of illness is often limited to the physical—to 'abnormalities in the structure and/or function of human organs or organ systems'[7] in an individual. These abnormalities

---

7. Pilch, *Healing in the New Testament*, 24.

are diagnosed in a laboratory and treated with drugs or surgery, with or without involvement of the patient, the patient's family, or the patient's community. The aim of treatment is to cure—and, if that is not possible, to stop—the progression of pathologies of the body so that the patient can live autonomously, without the need for anyone else.

"By contrast, in Jesus's time, illness was understood as whatever robs a person of a sense of wellbeing," Sophia added. "Even today this is the understanding of illness in the eighty percent of the world that lacks Western biomedicine."[8]

"If we're not talking about a condition that can be diagnosed and cured by biomedical treatments, what are we talking about?" Benjamin asked.

"We are talking about illnesses that are caused by what Pope Francis often refers to as 'the globalization of indifference,'" Sophia said. "Human indifference, the wanton abdication of any responsibility for the other, runs rampant in the world. It is the cause of all types of sicknesses, including a growing number of biomedical diseases."

"So, we can say that an important part of our challenge is to help those we serve embrace a more holographic understanding of illness and healing," Benjamin reflected.

"Yes," Sophia replied, "to help others (and ourselves) learn to see the connections and care about them, *even by our preaching*."

V.

"Our fourth and final pylon is S for _spoken_," Sophia began.

"Of course it's spoken," Benjamin interjected. "It's preaching, after all!"

"So it would seem," Sophia laughed, "but there is more to this than we might think."

Sophia's demeanor became more serious as she continued. "Actually, Benjamin, the _spoken_ pylon is the most mystical of all

---

8. Pilch, *Healing in the New Testament*, 22.

four pylons. We have come to the place where we must consider how God works through the preacher—through *any* human who builds a bridge between *head* and *heart*—to transform and heal our world," she said.

"Okay," Benjamin shrugged. "You've got me."

"In Genesis 1:27, we learn that God created us, male and female, in the divine image and likeness. Have you ever thought deeply about what that means?" Sophia asked.

Benjamin admitted, "I really haven't . . ."

"It's an important question," Sophia prodded gently.

"If I had to say anything, I'd say that each person has the indwelling Holy Spirit," Benjamin ventured.

"That's true," Sophia said, "but there is more."

She paused then spoke slowly: "Of all creation, only humans have been given the gift to live beyond inevitability. Only humans are able to deeply contemplate what is happening and then use language—the spoken word—to change reality."

Sophia sat quietly, letting Benjamin absorb her words, before saying softly, "This is the gift of languaged reflectivity."

* * * *

"Catholic theologian Sandra Schneiders writes extensively about language," Sophia continued. "Schneiders describes language as 'the primary symbolic activity of human beings.' Through language, she writes, 'the otherwise imperceptible reality of thought and feeling is expressed.' This expression spurs healing by 'challenging the hearer to engage that which is brought forth in word and to be changed by that encounter.'"[9]

"This is interesting," Benjamin reflected. "Although there is a great deal of evidence that animals—even sea-life and plants and the trees around us—can think and communicate with each other at some level, they do not have the ability to speak in a way that brings about *extensive* change."

"Extensive change . . ." Sophia echoed. "Tell me more."

9. Schneiders, *The Revelatory Text*, 139.

"I know that pets can change reality for their owners—that a cat of a diabetic can tell when its care-giver's blood sugar is falling to a dangerously low level and alert the person to get food," Benjamin said, "and I see how dogs offer great comfort to their caregivers or to patients being treated for cancer. But you are right: even if animals are aware of large-scale danger or sadness, they do not have the language to reverse the situation."

"They do not have the language," Sophia repeated, stressing every syllable.

"Awareness of illness by itself is not enough to bring about healing. This awareness must be elevated to human consciousness through the spoken word—put more simply, through the act of *naming pain*. Dominican homiletician Mary Catherine Hilkert observes that 'the first step toward overcoming suffering is finding language that leads one out of the prison of suffering.'

"Nevertheless, while naming pain is essential, it is not the final word. For healing to happen, the naming of pain *must* be followed by *kerygma* (proclamation of the Good News that the cross is not the final word). Kerygma gives us hope and assurance of resurrection, even from the height of the cross or the shadow of the grave. As Hilkert stresses, 'the embrace of pain through the process of lament [that is, of naming pain] is possible . . . only because one has hope that the future can be different.'[10]

"Pope Francis makes an important point in *Evangelii Gaudium*, his document on preaching, when he warns us against getting so caught up in pain that we lose sight of resurrection hope," Sophia added.

* * * *

Benjamin fell silent. Vivid images of some of the suffering he had witnessed during his year as a priest played in his mind as he watched the beginning sunset.

"It is easy to lose sight of resurrection hope," he finally said.

---

10. Hilkert, *Naming Grace*, 119.

"Yes, it is," Sophia said gently. "God knows it is! And I think that is what Pope Francis was saying when he wrote, 'There are Christians whose lives seem like Lent without Easter. I realize of course that joy is not expressed the same way at all times of life, especially in moments of great difficulty. Joy adapts and changes, but it always endues, even as a flicker of light born out of our personal certainty that, when everything is said and done, we are infinitely loved.'"[11]

* * * *

Orange-red streaks now painted the sky; soon it would be dark.

"I would like to share a powerful idea about Christian preaching," Sophia said. "Think about this statement tonight: Christian preaching brings the divine love story into consciousness where it may be encountered, engaged, and embraced. It offers others a new and healing vision of reality.

"Mary Catherine Hilkert quotes Methodist clergyman Stephen Crites: 'To offer others a new vision of reality, a new way of understanding and interpreting life, is in fact to offer them a new life. . . . conversion occurs through a new awakening of consciousness: not only [one's] past and future, but the very cosmos in which [one] lives is strung in a new way.'"[12]

VI.

"My head is spinning!" Benjamin observed.

"We *have* covered a great deal," Sophia agreed. "Would you like to tell me what you heard?"

"Yes—let me see if I've got this," he began. "Healing is a process of bridge-building. The bridge we are building aims to connect the *head*—the human spirit, where thinking and choosing occur—to the *heart* . . . God Who Is Love.

---

11. Francis, *Evangelii Gaudium*, paragraph 6.
12. Hilkert, *Naming* Grace, 31.

FOUR PYLONS OF A SPIRITUALITY OF PREACHING THAT HEALS

"Like most bridges, *this* bridge rests on pylons. There are four pylons for preaching that heals. They can be remembered by an acrostic: G/IHS—the <u>G</u>ospel of Jesus, the Christ, <u>i</u>ntentionally and <u>h</u>olographically <u>s</u>poken.

"With the Gospel at the center, we intentionally try to discern the particular illness Jesus is addressing and then consider how that illness is impacting those to whom we will preach. We take a holographic view of illness as anything that destroys a person's wellbeing and robs their ability to love—self, the other (including any part of God's creation), and God.

"Then, in preaching, we name the pain out loud and speak a vision of a new reality—hope of life in greater love," he paused. "Is that it?"

"That's it," Sophia said. "G/IHS, the four pylons of a spirituality of preaching that heals."

* * * *

As they got up to leave, Benjamin asked, "When and where will we meet tomorrow?"

"How about 9 a.m. at the pond called Lost Cypress, near the fishing dock?" Sophia suggested. "We are going to delve into a fascinating area—human anthropology."

"Human anthropology?" Benjamin puzzled.

"Our understanding about how God has created human beings so that language—*even* Sunday preaching—can bring about healing," Sophia smiled.

— Interlude —

Reflection on the Importance of Knowing How Things Are Put Together

Benjamin arrived at Lost Cypress hours before his meeting with Sophia. He'd awakened to cool pre-light dawn, grabbed an orange and cereal bars, filled a thermos with coffee, and headed to the fishing dock—to his mind, one of the most tranquil places in the world—to watch the sunrise.

Enveloped in beauty, Benjamin let his thoughts wander. It seemed odd that only five years earlier, few people knew this pond existed. Despite its proximity to the farmhouse, the pond had been obscured by a dense thicket of pines. A prickly undergrowth made it even less accessible. It wasn't until Benjamin's father had decided to resuscitate <u>his</u> father's dream of a recreational nature preserve that a path had been cut to the pond. Only then had its long-concealed beauty revealed itself.

Benjamin had helped build the dock. He remembered nailing thick two-by-twelve boards to a frame to create a twelve-square-foot platform which was positioned over buoyant 55-gallon drums. The dock now floated gently next to the shore, tethered in place by ropes tied to sturdy posts and a ramp for easy access. Wooden siderails on the dock and ramp kept guests from falling into the pond.

As Benjamin recalled building the dock, a thought crossed his mind: knowing how the dock was built made it possible to maintain it, keep it safe, and make repairs when necessary.

INTERLUDE: KNOWING HOW THINGS ARE PUT TOGETHER

Speaking out loud he exclaimed, "So <u>this</u> is why human anthropology matters! It really <u>is</u> important to know how things are put together!"

He was startled when Sophia approached from behind, "Yes, it <u>is</u> important . . ."

— Chapter 4 —

Human Anthropology

The 'Anatomy' of Preaching that Heals

I.

Joining Benjamin on the dock, Sophia continued, "Human anthropology seeks to understand how God has wired us, how illness originates and grows, and why illness is always a spiritual matter. It also helps us combat it."

Pausing, she added, "A doctor trained in Western 'scientific' medicine wouldn't attempt to diagnose or treat a biomedical condition without first understanding human anatomy. Essentially, human anthropology is *our* 'anatomy' for healing, *even by our preaching.*"

Benjamin sat quietly, absorbing the idea.

"When you said we'd be talking about human anthropology last night, I was confused," he confessed.

"Confused?" Sophia asked.

"Confused," Benjamin repeated. "At first I'd wondered whether human anthropology and congregational analysis were the same things."

"And?" Sophia prodded.

"I've come to realize they're *not*," he said. "Congregational analysis is a preaching best practice that considers the assembly to be addressed *before* preparing the sermon or homily. Human anthropology looks at a single person."

"Correct," Sophia said. "A single person: the zero ground for all healing."

Catching Benjamin's eye, she asked, "Do you mind if I go into teaching mode?"

"I expected it," he smiled.

II.

"There are many approaches to human anthropology," Sophia began. "We are going to look at a *theotic* anthropology.[1] This viewpoint holds that God has created humans in the divine image and likeness, not so that we can *become* gods, but so that we can respond to grace to become who God has created us to be.

"As we've briefly considered, God has created us in the divine image and likeness with the ability to live beyond inevitability. Of all creation, we alone can contemplate what is happening and, when we discern illness, use the language of word and deed to change the future. This gift—this *languaged reflectivity*—makes it possible for us to serve as conduits of God's love. It makes it possible for us to heal, *even by our preaching.*"

* * * *

Sophia continued, "Dominican preacher-theologian Carla Mae Streeter details the anthropology we are going to consider in her book, *Foundations of Spirituality: A Systematic Approach: The Human and the Holy.*[2] As Streeter explains, although religion has often looked at the human as a dualistic being with a physical body (too often regarded as 'evil') and an unseen spirit (regarded as 'good'), the human actually is a 'triple-composite' *whole* with an Organism, Psyche, and Spirit.[3]

1. Helminiak, *Religion and the Human Sciences*, 7–10; chapter 2.
2. Although my discussion of the triple-composite human and the emotions draws from Streeter's work, it also includes ideals from Helminiak and Larry Dossey as well as my own insights.
3. Streeter, *Foundations of Spirituality*, 48–49.

"From the moment of conception, life energy from God orchestrates the unfolding of a recognizable human, beginning with the Organism, the human's physicality. This energy comes through the Psyche (which, among other things, is an energy field). It will continue to fuel the human throughout life to death. As the human matures, this energy presses the human to develop the unique operations of the human Spirit—thinking and choosing.

Benjamin interrupted, "I am struggling to picture this triple-composite human."

"Let's move to the picnic table so I can draw a diagram," Sophia suggested.

* * * *

HUMAN ANTHROPOLOGY

THE WONDROUS HUMAN:
The Anatomy of Spiritual Transformation

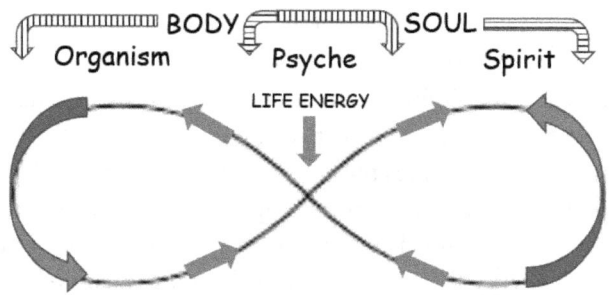

Organism:
(Organs, skin, bones, systems: all materiality that makes us identifiable humans)
Local:
(Lives in time and space)
Operations:
• Interacts with five senses
• Accumulates memories
Main Concerns:
• Biological health;
• Survival

Psyche:
(God's energy that fuels us)
Grounded in the Organism
Operations:
• Stores memories (Memories are accumulated by the Organism, including suppressed memories)
• Forms images
• Imagines; fantasizes; dreams
Main Concern:
• Comfort

Spirit:
(Consciousness):
(The seat of human intellect & will; the zero ground of spiritual transformation)
Nonlocal:
(Lives outside of time and space)
Operations:
• Thinking
• Choosing
Main Concern:
• Authenticity

EMOTIONS:
(Energy 'motors' that alert us to our state of wellbeing or illness)

SPONTANEOUS EMOTIONS:
Love   Hate
Desire   Aversion
Joy   Sorrow

CONSIDERED EMOTIONS:
Courage   Fear
Hope   Despair
+/- Anger

This diagram draws from Streeter's *Foundations of Spirituality*, Helminiak's *Religion and the Human Sciences*, and Dossey's *Healing Words*. The title, The Wondrous Human, is from Streeter.

Producing a large drawing pad and a marker, Sophia wrote **The Wondrous Human** at the top of a blank page. "This is the term Streeter uses to describe the human," she explained, "and, when you think about it, the way God has created us truly *is* wondrous."

Under the words, Sophia drew a large infinity sign, the number 8 resting on its side.

"Think of the infinity sign as a symbol for this human," she said. "The center cross-point between the two loops is the Psyche, which constantly provides the energy that fuels human life."

Over the center cross-point, Sophia wrote **Psyche** and drew an arrow with downward and upward points: "This arrow reminds us that the energy that fuels life comes from, and connects us to, God." In small letters, she wrote **Life Energy** over the arrow.

"Now, we move to the loops," Sophia said. Over the loop on the left, she wrote **Organism**, and over the loop on the right, **Spirit**.

"But what about the idea of body and soul?" Benjamin asked. "How do they fit in?"

"Good question," Sophia said. "Streeter defines the body as Organism plus Psyche and the soul as Psyche plus Spirit." On the diagram, she centered the word **Body** over **Organism** and **Psyche**, and the word **Soul** over **Psyche** and **Spirit**.

"It's important to remember that each part—the Organism, Psyche, and Spirit—works synchronously, with each performing specific operations *in relation to* and *essential for* the whole," Sophia said, drawing directional arrows on the infinity symbol to indicate synchronicity. "However, for the sake of clarity, we will consider each part separately, beginning with the Organism."

III.

"The Organism is our physicality—the biological organs, skin and bones, systems, and every physical part that makes us recognizable human beings. When animated by psychic energy, this living Organism, this *body*, can interact in the world," Sophia began.

"The living Organism interacts through the five senses—seeing, hearing, touching, tasting, and smelling. Through these interactions, it accumulates sensate feeling memories that will influence the human in every way, *physically*, *psychically*, and *spiritually*.[4]

"Living in time and space, the Organism is *local*.[5] It is subject to aging, sickness, injury, and death," Sophia added. "Its main concerns are biological health and survival."[6]

Under **Organism** on her diagram, she wrote **Local**, **Interacts (Five Senses)**, **Accumulates Memories**, and **Main Concerns: Biological Health and Survival**.

* * * *

"We move on to the Psyche," Sophia continued. "In addition to being an energy field rooted in the Organism, the Psyche performs critical operations of its own.

"First and foremost, the Psyche 'affects, absorbs, and records bodily functioning in psychic memory.' This includes experiences that are easy to recall, those we suppress because they are too painful to remember, and those of which the human is not consciously aware.

"Psychic memory enables the human to *image* (form mental pictures); *imagine* (link these pictures together), *fantasize* (link images together in a new way), and *dream*.[7] It also enables one other critical operation—*emotions*—that we will return to shortly.

"The Psyche's main concern is comfort,"[8] she added.

Under **Psyche**, Sophia wrote **(Grounded in Organism)**, **Memory, Imaging, Imagining, Fantasizing, Dreaming**, and **Main Concern: Comfort**.

---

4. Streeter, *Foundations of Spirituality*, 22.
5. Dossey, *Reinventing Medicine*, 19.
6. Helminiak, *Religion and the Human Sciences*, 29.
7. Streeter, *Foundations of Spirituality*, 56–57.
8. Helminiak, *Religion and the Human Sciences*, 29.

* * * *

"The third part of the human is Spirit," Sophia said. "The Spirit, also known as *consciousness*, is the seat of the human's intellect and will—thinking and choosing. The Spirit is *nonlocal*, meaning that it exists outside of time and space and therefore is eternal."

"Essentially, the process of healing—of building a bridge between *head* and *heart*—involves helping the human change the way he or she is thinking and choosing," Sophia continued. "It is a gentle process of conversion that draws upon the human capacity of languaged reflexivity to reorient the intellect and will to God."

"How can preachers help?" Benjamin asked.

"By offering the person a new basis for thinking and choosing," Sophia answered. "The new way will always point to a greater good—to love. It will always strengthen the *head*-to-*heart* bridge."

Benjamin sat quietly, absorbing the information.

"The main concern of the human Spirit is authenticity,"[9] Sophia added. "It is the highest attribute of the human who is living as God created him or her to be."

Under **Spirit** on her diagram, she wrote the words (**Consciousness**), **Nonlocal**, **Thinking and Choosing**, and **Main Concern: Authenticity**.

"Without much difficulty, we can recognize people who are living authentically," she added. "Authentic people exude a deep and palpable connection between the *head* and *heart* that is attractive and transformative. They live hopefully, confidently, and fearlessly in love, with increasing trust in God Who, after all, *is* love."

IV.

"There is one other operation of the Psyche that I've saved until now—the *emotions*," Sophia said. "Streeter describes the emotions

---

9. Helminiak, *Religion and the Human Sciences*, 29.

as 'powerful energy motors'[10] and, in every sense, this is precisely what they are," Sophia stressed.

"Think of emotions as an internal Emergency Alert System. They well up from the Psyche and fire off without warning, capturing our attention (even if only for an instant) and alerting us to illness or wellbeing," she explained.

"Saint Thomas Aquinas described eleven emotions. Six are identified as 'spontaneous emotions' because, as Streeter writes, they 'arise *spontaneously* from information that is sensed bodily.'[11] We can think of these emotions as three pairs of opposites: *love* and *hate*, *desire* and *aversion*, and *joy* and *sorrow*," she continued.

Under the **Organism** and **Psyche** columns on her diagram, Sophia wrote:

Spontaneous Emotions:

Love	**Hate**
Desire	**Aversion**
Joy	**Sorrow**

"The remaining five emotions are 'considered emotions.' They are associated with the Spirit because they emerge with thought," Sophia continued.

"Considered emotions relate to perceived threats that prompt a *flight*, *fight*, or *freeze* response. They also are seen in expressions of guilt, shame, or blame. These emotions include two pairs of opposites, *courage* and *fear*, and *hope* and *despair*, and *anger*,[12] which I've come to believe is its *own* opposite," she said.

"Anger: the opposite of itself?" Benjamin asked.

Sophia affirmed, "Yes, because, on the one hand, anger can alert us to grave injustices and threats to the greater good—a first step in addressing or preventing harm to ourselves, to others,

---

10. Streeter, *Foundations of Spirituality*, 57.
11. Streeter, *Foundations of Spirituality*, 58.
12. Streeter, *Foundations of Spirituality*, 58.

or any part of creation. On the other hand, anger can alert us to threats to our selfish interests that are working against the greater good—for example, anger that arises from envy or jealousy."

Under the **Psyche** and **Spirit** columns on her diagram, Sophia added:

Considered Emotions:

Courage	**Fear**
Hope	**Despair**

+/-**Anger**

"There is one thing you need to remember about emotions, Benjamin," Sophia said gently. "We must never ignore them because they are powerful mirrors of our state of wellbeing. Streeter writes beautifully about this: 'To ignore emotion in spiritual development is to court trouble. . . . Not dealt with, it . . . can cripple intelligence and paralyze choice.'"[13]

* * * *

"May I have the diagram?" Benjamin asked.

Sophia handed the sheet to him, and Benjamin placed it on the table and studied it. Finally, he exclaimed, "This is *packed*!"

"What particularly are you noticing?" Sophia asked.

"What strikes me most is how fragile and vulnerable humans are," Benjamin began. "The idea that we *absorb* and *record* absolutely everything into memory—even things we are not consciously aware of—is huge!"

"It *is* huge," Sophia echoed. "We begin to see how *everything*—especially negative things like unkind gestures, throw-away comments, and misunderstood jokes—can influence how a person thinks and chooses, not just for a moment, but for life."

---

13. Streeter, *Foundations of Spirituality*, 58.

Benjamin said quietly, "When I think about it, I first started to understand my preaching was a problem not because anyone said anything directly to me, but because of the subtle body language of people in the pews."

"And how did this affect you?" Sophia asked.

"At first, I felt gut-punched, and then—over time, with thought—like I was spiraling downward," Benjamin replied. "The uneasiness—the *pain*—became overwhelming."

"A downward spiral: gripped by an illness that affected every part of you—Organism, Psyche, and Spirit," Sophia said, "and you didn't know how you would recover."

"Right," Benjamin said, "but until *now*, I hadn't thought of it as an illness."

"You've brought up a key point, Benjamin," Sophia said. "How we define illness determines how we look at health *and* approach healing."

Pausing, she asked, "Because this is so important, I leave it to you: would you like to continue, or would you rather take a break?"

"I want to go on," Benjamin exclaimed without hesitation.

V.

"You mentioned that you hadn't thought of your preaching experience as an illness *until now*, Benjamin," Sophia observed, "so let me ask: how have you defined illness?"

"Mostly as something that affects the body," he replied.

"That's how most of us who live in so-called 'scientific' Westernized cultures think of illness," Sophia said. "Our understanding is mainly limited to the biological dimension of the human, the Organism. Our culture tends to downplay anything that can't be diagnosed in a laboratory and treated with surgery or drugs."

She added. "Quoting H. Tristram Engelhardt, Biblical anthropologist John Pilch describes Western medicine's understanding of health as 'the ability to perform those functions which allow the organism to maintain itself, other things being equal, in the range of activity open to most members of the species (for example, within two standard deviations from the norm) which are conducive to the maintenance of the species.'"[14]

Benjamin winced, "This sounds like a gross reduction."

"It certainly is a reduction, and it certainly is gross," Sophia agreed. "This understanding has had tragic ramifications in our culture. Many people think of health as the physical ability to live independently, without the need for or the concern of others. It is the antithesis of the communion to which God calls us."

"This explains something I see all the time—something that bothers me," Benjamin said. "I've noticed that even people with deep religious faith dread becoming a burden to others and—if we have the stomach to admit it—being burdened by others. It seems that death is preferable to inconvenience, even when a loved one is involved."

"Tragically true," Sophia sighed. "When we limit our definition of health to independent, autonomous functioning of the living Organism, how can we possibly appreciate the fullness of the Gospel and the totality of Jesus's healings?"

Pausing, she added, "Jesus's healings align with the World Health Organization's definition of health as a 'state of complete physical, mental [psychic], and social wellbeing and not merely the absence of disease and infirmity.'[15] They were always comprehensive, addressing the needs of the fully-integrated human—Organism, Psyche, and Spirit. They also were communal. Jesus recognized what we tend to overlook—that *illness* not only affects the person who is afflicted, but those close to the person, and, in many cases, those whose actions or neglect are *causing* the illness."

"I can't imagine what a state of *complete* wellbeing would look like," Benjamin mused. "Is it even possible?"

"With grace, yes!" Sophia assured him. "Let's look at the dimensions of wellbeing."

---

14. Pilch, *Healing in the New Testament*, 24.
15. Pilch, *Healing in the New Testament*, 24.

VI.

She continued, "In his classic, *Basic Types of Pastoral Counseling: Resources for the Ministry of Healing and Growth*, Howard Clinebell presents a model of seven interconnected dimensions that influence a person's sense of wholeness and wellbeing.[16] Interestingly, this model is as valid for non-Western cultures as it is for Western scientific cultures.

"I thought this might be helpful, Benjamin," Sophia said, producing a diagram of Clinebell's model. The model showed six ovals surrounding a larger central oval. Each oval was connected to the center and every other oval as well.

---

16. Clinebell, *Basic Types of Pastoral Counseling*, 30.

The Healthy Human: Clinebell's Seven Dimensions of Wellbeing

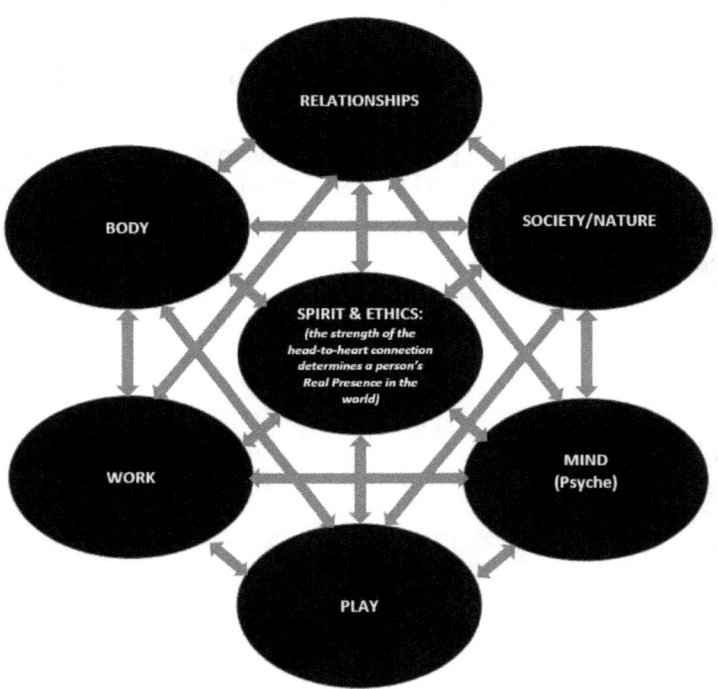

"At the center of the drawing is '*spirit and ethics*,'" Sophia said. "Clinebell describes *spirit and ethics* as 'the unifying, integrating core around which all other dimensions interact . . . the axle on which all other dimensions—*mind, body, relationships, work, play,* and *society/nature*—turn, more or less effectively.'"[17]

Benjamin studied the diagram. "Why is *spirit and ethics* at the center?" he asked.

"Because—Clinebell writes—'The strength, integrity, and wholeness of this [*spirit and ethics*] dimension profoundly influence people's overall wellbeing and how well they function in other

17. Clinebell, *Basic Types of Pastoral Counseling*, 10.

areas of their lives. . . . The spiritual key to whole-person wellness is a trustful, nourishing, growing relationship with the divine Spirit—the ultimate source of all life,'"[18] Sophia replied.

* * * *

Looking thoughtful, Benjamin summarized, "So, our Spirit (our consciousness) *and* the ethics that flow from it influence wellbeing, for better or worse."

"Yes," Sophia affirmed, "A person's relationship with God—the *head*-to-*heart* connection—determines the person's sense of wellbeing. Is the person's *spirit and ethics* dimension centered on a graced relationship with God that is drawing the person to ever-greater love? Are the person's thoughts and actions guided by this relationship? Or has the *spirit and ethics* dimension faded to the background, becoming less important than other dimensions or having no importance at all?"

Benjamin observed, "Even though the *spirit and ethics* dimension is at the center, the other dimensions *also* impact the whole."

"Continuously," Sophia agreed. "*All* of the dimensions are fully integrated and continually impact one another. You have only to look at your own life to see how a change in any one area affects every other area, Benjamin. And it doesn't matter whether that change is as life-shattering as the onset of a chronic illness, the death of a loved one, or questioning your vocation, or as pleasant as achieving a long-term goal.

"Moreover, *any* dimension can come to dominate the whole. We all know people whose lives are centered on the *work* dimension and doing whatever it takes to get ahead on the job, even if it means hurting other people. Or on the *social* dimension with an overarching life driver of being popular, admired, and invited to the 'right' parties. Or on the body and physical perfection.

"If we're not on guard, any dimension can become a false god that consumes our life and weakens or breaks the *head-to-heart* connection," she added.

18. Clinebell, *Basic Types of Pastoral Counseling*, 10.

* * * *

"Is it even possible to be healthy?" Benjamin asked. "After all, it's unlikely that *all* dimensions will ever be in a state of perfect wellbeing and balance, guided by a God-centered *spirits and ethics* dimension."

"Highly unlikely," Sophia agreed, "and yet, as Clinebell discovered, wellbeing does not depend upon every dimension operating optimally and in perfect balance. Clinebell found that even physical health—although helpful—is not necessary for wholeness. He writes, 'A remarkable fact about humans is that most persons with major, even multiple, disabilities have the capacity to integrate their physical limitations and develop the potentialities for intellectual acumen, creative productivity, and spiritual maturity.'"[19]

Benjamin reflected, "One of my homebound parishioners is widowed. Her children live some distance away, and she lives alone. Her physical disabilities would be crippling to most people. Nevertheless, she lives an incredibly rich, meaningful, and joyful life. She spends hours each day praying the rosary for other people, closely follows the news, and is one of the most curious people I've ever met.

"She radiates peace and joy. *I* feel better whenever I visit," he added.

"It sounds like she has a strong *head*-to-*heart* connection," Sophia observed.

"But how did she develop it?" Benjamin asked. "How do I? And how can I bring this healing to others through my preaching? We need to talk about this."

"But not now," Sophia said. "It's time to take a break."

Benjamin persisted, "When can we meet again?"

"Let's meet at 4:30 this afternoon at the main entrance to the pine forest," Sophia replied. "We'll begin looking at the four pylons of a spirituality of preaching that heals, starting with the Gospels, our best handbook for healing.

"Bring a water bottle," she added. "We'll walk while we talk."

---

19. Clinebell, *Basic Types of Pastoral Counseling*, 55.

— Chapter 5 —

Pylon One: Gospel

Lessons for Preaching that Heals

I.

Benjamin arrived at the entrance to the pine forest at 4:30 p.m. sharp. Despite the late-afternoon summer heat, the forest was bearable, even pleasant. Sunlight streaked the soft pine-needle floor, and a gentle breeze rustled through the treetops.

The pine forest covered a third of the farm. Shortly after Benjamin's grandfather acquired the farm in the late 1950s, he'd planted 50,000 Eastern white and red pine seedlings over terrain that sloped down to a creek near the farm's southern edge. Now, the trees—most of them well over seventy feet tall—stood rigidly upright like soldiers at attention, straining to drink the sun. Their branch-and-needle crowns formed a protective awning over the forest.

Sophia was waiting just inside.

"We're going to explore what the Gospels teach us about healing," she greeted him. "Would you like to walk while we talk?"

Without hesitation, Benjamin said, "Let's go."

* * * *

As the two started down the main path, Benjamin began, "You mentioned a couple of days ago that the Gospels *in their entirety* are about healing, not just the stories about specific cures."

"Correct," Sophia said. "*Every* part of the Gospels tells us something about healing. In fact, Jesus chose to initiate the reign of God by healing. His method was preaching with every word and deed. This is why the Gospels truly are our ultimate handbook for preaching that heals."

"I've never thought about the Gospels this way," Benjamin admitted.

"Most of us haven't," Sophia said, "It's especially challenging for those of us who live in Western scientific cultures and limit our definition of illness to physical sickness. To grasp the full significance of Gospel healing, we have to understand illness differently—as any condition that robs a person of wellbeing. Healing restores wellbeing."

"Restores wellbeing," Benjamin mused. "Easy words, but what do they really mean?"

"Good question," Sophia said. "Wellbeing is a sense that we—along with *all* creation—are loved and of infinite value, no matter what. It recognizes that we—along with *all* creation—are embedded in the divine mystery of God, who is absolute love."

"*Embedded?*" Benjamin asked.

"Embedded," Sophia affirmed. "Every breath we take should remind us of our integral connection to God, the Uncreated Cause of all that is who loves us beyond our wildest imagination. Every breath should remind us of God's Spirit of love that dwells within us. Wellbeing comes with recognizing and living into God's love. It's the only thing that can bring us what we crave—lasting satisfaction, meaning, joy, and peace.

"The trouble is, it's easy to get sidetracked by selfish interests (ours or someone else's) that put possessions, power, and prestige *before* love. Disordered interests turn us away from love—from God. When this happens, all types of illnesses—physical, psychological, and spiritual—occur.

"In the Gospels, Jesus teaches us how to recognize illness and restore wellbeing through preaching that heals," she added. "Are you ready to learn to read them *differently?*"

"I am," Benjamin said.

II.

"Our first challenge is to learn to read the Gospels *beyond* ourselves," Sophia began.

"*Beyond* ourselves?" Benjamin asked. "Is this even possible?"

"Absolutely!" Sophia exclaimed. "Do you remember our discussion about location—the idea that what we see depends on where we stand?"

"Yes. That first day on the bridge," Benjamin recalled.

"Learning to read *beyond* ourselves is crucial because we tend to assume that others see things just like we do. We not only do this in everyday life, but we also project our assumptions on people who live in entirely different cultures and times, including the first followers of Jesus and the communities for whom the Gospels were written," Sophia said. "To approach *any* text *beyond* ourselves, we first have to understand where we stand."

Stopping on the trail, she looked at Benjamin and asked, "So, Benjamin, where are *you* standing?"

Benjamin returned her gaze. "Well, I'm an ordained Roman Catholic priest. I'm in my late 20s," he began. "Well educated with a strong background in theology. From a tight-knit, upper-middle-class family. I was baptized as an infant and grew up in the church I serve, learning the stories, and living the tradition.

"I've spent nearly half of my life discerning my call to be a priest and preparing for it, with the full backing of people I care about. My vocation is very demanding, but my life is structured so I can meet the demands. I have mentors and a support system to help.

"I also have the time and resources to do other things I like: getting together with friends, taking vacations, hiking, and camping out.

"I'll never have to worry about job security. And, although I care for the people I serve, I don't have a wife and kids—something I sometimes regret.

"My housing's taken care of, I get a stipend for other living expenses *and* a salary, and I have insurance and a pension. All of my material needs are met. I live in relative peace and security, free from fear," Benjamin stopped.

"Go on," Sophia pressed.

"Is there more?" Benjamin asked.

"Yes!" Sophia emphasized. "Look in a mirror!"

Thinking for a moment, Benjamin added sheepishly, "I'm a celibate white American male of Northern European descent."

"Extremely important! When it comes to reading beyond ourselves, we can take *nothing* for granted—especially things that bespeak a position of privilege and power!" Sophia exclaimed.

"This is where you stand. Your social location," she added.

Resuming their walk, they quickly reached the end of the main path and had a choice: go left and weave down a steep embankment to the creek and a sandbar, or turn right and hike through a rugged, hilly terrain replete with brambles and swampy low-points.

Resolutely, they turned right.

* * * *

Sophia let Benjamin mull over his social location as they started down the farm's most treacherous path. They had to watch where they were walking to keep from tripping on fallen branches or brushing against sticker bushes.

After several minutes of silent hiking, Sophia asked, "Now, another question—a big one. How do you think *your* social location compares to that of the people you serve . . . the people in your parish?"

"Ouch!" Benjamin grimaced. "I hate to admit it, but there are enormous differences."

He began a painful litany: "I don't know what it's like to be responsible for a wife and kids or to worry about things like putting food on the table, job security, affording insurance, or paying for other basics. Or saving for college (assuming college would even be in the realm of possibility). I don't know what it's like to see *my* child in trouble: *suffering*.

"I can't imagine having cancer and watching my body being ravaged by disease and medical treatments. Or being widowed and alone, without natural day-to-day contacts.

"Or *not* being solidly middle-class. Living in substandard housing in a dangerous part of town, or being homeless. Living paycheck to paycheck on minimum wage without benefits or health insurance, or trying to get by without a job at all. Having no support system. Being lonely. Trying my best to make ends meet, but knowing the deck is stacked against me from the get-go." His voice trailed off.

"This is using your imagination to go beyond yourself—to put yourself in someone else's shoes," Sophia said. "Reading *beyond* ourselves requires using our imagination to enter into the experience of others at a *gut* level. Unless we *feel* their challenges, pain, and suffering, we'll probably miss the need for healing."

Pausing, she said, "I think we're ready to consider the experience of Jesus's first followers and the communities addressed in the Gospels."

III.

"You already know much of what we're going to discuss," Sophia began, "but I'm asking you to look at it differently. I'm asking you to use your imagination and your experience of love to *engage* in the world of Jesus and his first followers.

"The people Jesus served were in dire need of healing. When Jesus began his ministry (at roughly your age, Benjamin), he was older than around 75 percent of the population. The people not only were younger, but they were looking at an additional decade or less of life expectancy.[1]

"Most people were sick and hungry. No matter how hard the typical man—the chief wage earner—worked, he could only meet two-thirds of his family's daily dietary needs. Women had to do

---

1. Malina and Rohrbaugh, *Social Science Commentary on the Synoptic Gospels*, 326–327.

whatever paid work they could to help their families ward off starvation and diseases related to hunger.²

"Unlike those of us in Western scientific cultures who value independence and want to control everything (including nature), Jesus lived in a world that understood the need for community and living in harmony with nature. Survival depended on it.

"Jesus served mostly poor, illiterate, and powerless Jewish peasants who lived in rural communities. They lived under the oppressive occupation of the Roman Empire. Even though the people could not earn enough to meet their own needs, they were forced to pay confiscatory taxes to Rome. They lived in fear, always in danger of brutal reprisal—literal bloodbaths—at the first hint of resistance.

"But there was more," Sophia continued. "Wealthier community members—among them, landowners and those who controlled fishing rights—often exploited their less advantaged neighbors. (Although we're familiar with the idea that landowners hired laborers to work in their fields and vineyards, we forget that fishing required a license and fishermen were obligated to share the catch with the grantor—sometimes to usurious extremes.)

"Can you imagine this, Benjamin?" Sophia asked.

"I can," he said thoughtfully.

"But the peasants' plight didn't stop there," she added.

* * * *

"Episcopal preacher David Urion writes that most of the people Jesus served lived under the domination of *two* empires—in addition to Imperial Rome, the Temple in Jerusalem," Sophia said. "Although we might think Rome and the Temple were worlds apart, Urion argues otherwise. *Both* imposed categories of *being* on people that labeled and divided them, and *both* depended on their subjects' allegiance to these categories."³

"Categories of *being*?" Benjamin mused.

2. Reid, *The Gospel of Luke*, lecture six.
3. Urion, *Compassion as a Subversive Activity*, 47.

"Categories of being," Sophia affirmed. "Like all empires, Rome and the Temple created 'in' and 'out' categories that became profoundly embedded in the culture.

"It's important to know that *every* empire establishes 'in' and 'out' categories of *being*. These categories are the basis for hierarchies of position and control. *Every* person in the empire is assigned to an 'in' class, a marginalized 'out' class, or worse, an altogether invisible subaltern class. (In our own culture, think about homeless families who live in cars. Because they're not sleeping on the street, it is easy to be blind to their existence.)

"It's especially interesting that even those who live at or beyond the margins tend to accept their categories without question," she added.

Coming to a particularly narrow and brambly section of the path, Benjamin and Sophia walked without talking for a while.

As they arrived at a clearing, Benjamin observed, "We live in a world of empires."

"Yes," Sophia agreed, "and they're not necessarily as large as Rome or the Temple. They can be as small as a single person or family group—*any* force that gains primacy over a person's spiritual operations of thinking and choosing."

* * * *

"*Every* empire, even those that begin with noble purposes, exists in a world of sin," Sophia said. "Selfish interests, greed, careerism, and disordered desires can easily take hold of people at every level. When this happens, the empire can devolve to the point that it oppresses and hurts the very people it originally hoped to serve."

"Is there a way to recognize a devolved empire?" Benjamin asked.

"There is," Sophia said. "Within every devolved empire, many people are more concerned about protecting their positions than serving the greater good. To maintain or strengthen their status, they reward lower-ranking people who support them, creating a beholden underclass driven by fear.

"Subjected underlings, in turn, may clamor to improve *their* status by ingratiating themselves to higher-ups. Living in fear of losing what they have or coming to believe they deserve nothing better, this underclass may become blind to gross injustices because 'that's just the way things are.' The pattern continues in a deadly, downward spiral. Ironically, go-along/get-along complicity of exploited people strengthens the empires that oppress them.

"Devolved empires divide and enslave people," Sophia continued, "and—as Jesus knew—they cause illness."

Benjamin interjected, "But, the Temple?"

"Even religious institutions," Sophia affirmed.

IV.

"You know that Jesus was a faithful Jew," Sophia began. "He was born into a family of faithful Jews and grew up immersed in the Jewish tradition—much the way you grew up in the Roman Catholic tradition, Benjamin. *Because* he understood and cared about Judaism, Jesus recognized attitudes, teachings, and practices that had seeped into his religion, seemingly becoming more important than God."

"Attitudes, teachings, and practices that were weakening the *spirit and ethics* center that connects humans to God—the *head*-to-*heart* connection," Benjamin said with new appreciation.

"And, in the weakening, causing illness," Sophia added.

"In Jesus's highly religious Jewish culture, many people believed that illness, sickness, or any type of affliction was a punishment from God for sin. Illness had severe religious and social repercussions. Many who were ill were excluded from religious activities and, if the illness was serious enough, from the community itself.

"There was no shortage of people ready to judge and condemn the sick instead of helping them. This included many religious leaders. It's what put Jesus at odds with them.

"Instead of judgment and condemnation, Jesus responded to illness with compassion," she said. "According to the Gospel of John, Jesus *refused* to judge."

* * * *

"As Morton Kelsey explains in *Healing and Christianity*, Jesus saw the common belief that illness was God's punishment for sin as 'tragically inadequate,'" Sophia continued. "Instead, Jesus followed the strand of Judaism that believed in the presence of evil spirits in the world—spirits that oppressed people, causing illnesses of every kind."[4]

Recalling the morning's conversation, Benjamin interjected, "By oppress, you are saying that evil in the world can overtake the human spirit (which is the same thing as human consciousness). It can affect a person's ability to think and choose. This is what Paul means in his Letter to the Romans: 'What I do, I do not understand. For I do not do what I want, but I do what I hate.'"

"It's one of my favorite passages too," Sophia said, "because it recognizes how deeply embedded sin can become—not just in people, but in empires. It can become *so* embedded that we're not even aware of it. When this happens, outside intervention is necessary for healing because the afflicted person or empire is blind to the illness."

Benjamin stopped and said thoughtfully, "Jesus said in the Gospel of Luke, 'The spirit of the Lord is upon me, because he has anointed me to bring glad tidings to the poor. He has sent me to proclaim liberty to captives and recovery of sight to the blind, to let the oppressed go free, and to proclaim a year acceptable to the Lord.'"

"I'm *getting* it!" he exclaimed.

"Before we go on, let's review one more thing: how Jesus's world looked at illness and healing," Sophia said.

---

4. Kelsey, *Healing and Christianity*, 48–50.

V.

"First-century Palestine did not look at illness and healing like we do," Sophia began. "We tend to limit our understanding of illness to biological anomalies that afflict an individual and can be diagnosed in a laboratory. We rely on science-based technologies, drugs, and/or surgery to treat the anomaly and leave this so-called 'healing' to doctors trained in biomedicine. While input from patients or their families may be helpful, it is not necessary for diagnosis or treatment.

"This is *not* the type of healing Jesus provided," she added, "and it's *not* the type of healing Pope Francis has challenged us to provide *even by our preaching*."

"What do we really understand about Jesus's healings?" Benjamin asked.

"We know Jesus was a Jewish folk healer who used healing methods that were understood by those he served—methods that are well within our reach and are still used by the 80 percent of our world that does not have science-based medicine,"[5] Sophia replied.

They arrived at a scenic overlook with two old stone-based bus-stop benches. "Let's sit here for a while," Sophia suggested.

"Good idea," Benjamin replied, taking a long drink from his water bottle.

* * * *

"Folk healing goes far beyond the impersonal care that is the focus of science-based medicine," Sophia began, going into teaching mode. "It uses our unique human gifts of *reflectivity* and *language* to restore wellbeing and, if possible, to confront and change 'empire' values, attitudes, and behaviors that caused the illness in the first place.

"By working with individuals who were ill and their communities, Jesus sought to restore *all* people—for that matter, *all*

---

5. Pilch, *Healing in the New Testament*, 22.

creation—to a state of wellbeing where authentic, *non-exploiting* relationships were possible."

"Relationships?" Benjamin asked.

"Illness severs relationships," Sophia explained. "Healing is *always* communal. It eliminates illness so that relationships can be restored.

"In Jesus's culture, the most valued relationship (at least nominally) was the relationship with God. Many illnesses in the Gospel involved one of three 'zones': the *eyes-heart* zone, the *ears-mouth* zone, and the *hands-feet* zone. Illnesses in each of these zones affected the person's relationship with God. *Eyes-heart* afflictions kept a person from knowing, understanding, and choosing God. *Ears-mouth* ailments kept the person from hearing and proclaiming the Good News. And *hands-feet* conditions made it impossible for the sufferer to follow Jesus with his or her whole being."[6]

"But what about illnesses that didn't affect one of the three zones?" Benjamin asked.

"These illnesses—seizures, fever, and other ailments for which the culture had no explanation—were attributed to demonic possession,"[7] Sophia replied.

"Like all folk healers, Jesus focused on the symptoms of an illness rather than the biological cause of sickness," she continued. "His goal was to understand and treat the sufferer's experience— the *reality* of the loss of wellbeing. The goal of treatment was to transform that reality; the method of treatment was the 'language' of words and deeds.

Pausing, she asked, "Would it be helpful to look at examples?"

"It would," Benjamin replied.

* * * *

"Let's start with Peter's mother-in-law," Sophia began. "She was unable to join her community at the synagogue because she was in bed with a fever. Since fevers were attributed to demonic

---

6. Harris, *We Speak the Word of the Lord*, 22.
7. Reid, *The Gospel of Luke*, lecture three.

possession, Jesus used the 'language' of exorcism for healing and restoration. Freed of the demons that caused her illness and separated her from the community, Peter's mother-in-law immediately got up and served."

"I've always been fascinated that she *got up and served*," Benjamin commented.

"Freely serving others is a powerful expression of love. It's a deep longing that flows from a relationship with God—from a strong *head*-to-*heart* connection," Sophia replied.

"Now, let's consider the man on the stretcher whose friends lowered him through the roof because he couldn't walk. What do you make of this, Benjamin?" she asked.

Benjamin reflected, "Given what you said about the three zones, the man's inability to walk meant that he couldn't follow Jesus. Something was standing in his way. His friends who carried the stretcher and lowered him through the roof knew it. Jesus knew it, too. Healing, which included the forgiveness of sins, relieved the man of his incapacitating burdens so he could resume his walk with God. It restored his *head*-to-*heart* connection."

They sat in silence while Benjamin absorbed the idea.

After some time, Sophia said, "Let's look at a case that people in our culture wouldn't even think of as healing: the Feeding of Five Thousand (not counting women and children).

"Even by today's standards, a crowd of five thousand is huge. But in Jesus's time, such a crowd was nearly unimaginable. Only about a hundred people lived in Jesus's hometown of Nazareth, and only 30 thousand in Jerusalem. And yet, when people *encountered* Jesus, they were healed! What's interesting about this feeding is that after Jesus blessed the loaves and fish, he had his disciples distribute the food to the crowd. Healing moved them from helplessness to a place of agency and initiative where they could feed each other.

"The Gospels explore virtually every type of human suffering. We too observe the *stasis* of illness—the tendency to fall under the spell of empires and settle for less than the abundance God offers. We too see resistance to healing by those whose wealth, power and prestige come from oppressing others. And—by paying careful attention, we too can learn to recognize illnesses that are as lethal today as they were in Jesus's time.

"We will never know *how* Jesus healed on this side of eternity," Sophia added, "but we can learn a great deal *from* Jesus through the Gospels, our best handbook for healing, *even by our preaching.*"

* * * *

When Benjamin finally headed back to the farmhouse several hours later, he felt that his heart would burst. As he and Sophia explored the Gospels as Jesus's handbook for preaching that heals, he'd had a growing sensation of being suspended in time and space. It was like catching a glimpse of his own soul. Benjamin was filled with a new sense of mission fueled by the boundless energy of exuberant hope. But there was more: he felt *changed*, and he *knew* his relationship with God had changed.

It was as if huge clods that stood between him and God had been lasered. Boulders of shame and guilt were not only rolled aside, but they were also crushed to smithereens. As the conduit between his *head* and *heart* cleared, Benjamin began to see how he could extend the healing Jesus offered to others, even—perhaps *especially*—through his preaching.

But now was not the time to contemplate what he had learned. Despite his sense of resurrection, Benjamin realized he was exhausted. The rose-tinged darkness confirmed what his body felt: it had been a long day—a challenging one. Tomorrow morning would be soon enough to reflect on his new insights.

Arriving at the farmhouse, Benjamin headed for the kitchen, made a sandwich, and opened a beer. After his quick meal, he headed upstairs, plopped down on his bed, and quickly fell asleep.

VI.

Benjamin was surprised that it was already 8 a.m. when he awoke. He couldn't remember when he'd slept so late—when he'd had the opportunity *and* been relaxed enough to take advantage of it.

He had the morning entirely free. Although Benjamin wasn't into journaling, he felt the need to capture key ideas from last evening's conversation. Challenged to explore the Gospels in a new and imaginative way for lessons on preaching that heals, Benjamin had noticed five things. He intended to jot them on a card and stash it in his Bible.

But first, he realized, he needed to address his *physical* hunger. Yesterday's cereal bars, fruit, and sandwich hadn't been enough to sustain his dawn-to-dusk outdoor activity. Benjamin headed to the kitchen and brewed fresh coffee, fried bacon and eggs, spooned yogurt into a bowl and topped it with blueberries and granola, and toasted a couple of pieces of thick country bread.

The morning was beautiful: sunny, in the low 70s. Benjamin piled his breakfast, a carafe of coffee, and writing materials on a large tray and headed for a shaded picnic table on the patio. Thanking God, he ate then began to write:

* * * *

Lesson One: Prayer is the conduit of healing.

Benjamin had known that Jesus prayed at critical times in his life, but he hadn't realized there were nearly *forty* mentions of Jesus's praying in the Gospels. Why so many? It occurred to him that the sheer number of mentions pointed to something significant: *Jesus was giving us, his disciples, a no-holds-barred model of prayer!*

Nothing was off-limits in Jesus's model. He prayed while making important decisions. He prayed before moments of self-revelation. He prayed prayers of thanksgiving over loaves and fish before feeding crowds of thousands. He prayed to consecrate bread and wine at the Last Supper. He prayed when he was being betrayed. He prayed in times of sadness. He prayed when he felt forsaken—when he felt his heart was breaking. He prayed for forgiveness of those who crucified him while he was hanging on the cross.

Prayer anchored Jesus's life, no matter what. It was a two-way conduit to God, the source of unchanging love. It was utterly worthy of Jesus's undivided attention—and, by his example, *ours*.

All healing comes from God, Benjamin realized. The preacher's ability to draw on Scripture to discern illness in a congregation, to identify a remedy, and to find the courage to articulate the balm of divine love: *Jesus was the bridge to God; prayer was the conduit.*

Jesus's prayer was never obligatory. It was relational. For humans prone to blinding illnesses of our own, it requires effort, discipline, perseverance, and patience. Benjamin remembered the words of one of his favorite mentors: *Our relationship with God develops the same way every other relationship does, with time and care.*

Benjamin cringed as he recalled *his* prayer in recent months. Often it (like much of his ministry) was little more than another perfunctory task on an endless checklist. He thought about his half-hearted attempts to practice the prayer of Lectio Divina in homily preparation in his parish office, with ringing phones, drop-in visitors, and gossiping staff just outside his door. This certainly wasn't the prayer Jesus modeled in the Gospels!

Recalling a wise pastor's comments that lapses in a preacher's prayer life always show up in the pulpit, Benjamin said under his breath, "Touché!"

* * * *

Lesson Two: Meet people where they are.

Benjamin knew that people followed Jesus wherever he went. Men, women, and children left their ordinary lives to seek him out. Crowds lined the roads to meet him. They climbed trees to see him. They left the Red Tent to touch him, the tax collector's booth to pursue him, their children's sick beds to appeal to him.

Thousands followed him to the mountain. One woman even crashed a banquet at the house of Simon-the-Pharisee.

But until now, Benjamin hadn't bothered to ask *why*?

Now in light of the Gospels, he understood. Without fail, Jesus responded to people in the most compelling way possible: he met them where they were. He refused to stone them and he didn't condemn them. He greeted them with acceptance, listened deeply with his whole being, and asked gentle questions that cut to the chase.

Slowly it occurred to Benjamin that meeting people where they are is the ultimate compliment and gift: real presence. This presence requires a person's undivided focus and deep listening. It makes every effort to suspend judgment and assumptions. Its total aim is to understand the experiences that have shaped the reality of individuals or groups.

Benjamin began to see that one of his shortcomings was a failure to meet people where they are. Hasty congregational analyses cloaked in personal judgments were not what Jesus modeled in the Gospels.

He blanched as he remembered celebrating Mass for grade school kids at the end of a week-long summer program, right before a long-anticipated water fight. In his exuberance, Benjamin had spoken for twenty minutes about an obscure tractate on the Sacred Heart. As he preached, he realized it was a mistake, but he couldn't help himself.

He began to see how ego and academic pride would always be a temptation.

Yet, even in the throes of doubt about his call to preach, Benjamin was enthralled by what he'd come to believe about God. He loved his church's well-thought-out doctrine and catechism. He believed the church knew what people needed in order to know, love, and serve God, and he saw himself as an agent.

He recalled asking Sophia, "Doesn't this count for something?"

She'd replied that *of course* it matters . . . *of course* preaching must be doctrinally correct. But then she added that *any* preaching will fall on deaf ears if you're not meeting people where they are. She'd added that preachers can offer healing only to the extent that they understand the events that have shaped the thinking and choosing of those they meet.

As they talked, Benjamin realized that meeting people where they are *never* meant compromising one's beliefs. However, it *did* require emulating Jesus. Without fail, Jesus met others within the constraints of their culture and gauged their ability to hear. He *never* offered adults the bland pabulum one feeds to infants, and he didn't force-feed children solids they couldn't digest.

While challenging the *afflicting*, Jesus responded to the afflicted with non-judgmental truth tempered with compassion. His gracious openness and reconciling love had the power to cut through thick patinas of guilt, shame, and denial, giving many who were suffering the courage to acknowledge and confront their illnesses at last.

For many, Benjamin saw, the experience of being met where they were was the first step toward healing.

* * * *

Lesson Three: Fund a new imagination.

Although Jesus met people where they were, he didn't leave them there. From his perspective of perfect love, he offered them an alternative to illness. His medium was the word flowing from contemplation and expressed in language and deed.

Jesus was a folk healer whose *every* word invited those who heard it to spiritual transformation. He offered people a new way of thinking and choosing that moved them from positions of subjugation *or* oppressive behavior to greater freedom and love. Jesus funded a new imagination—one that people were free to accept or reject.

With Sophia's gentle guidance, Benjamin began to see familiar Gospel stories differently. With *every* story, *every* parable, and *every* word, Jesus invited those he encountered to a place of healing, encouraging them to excise areas of blindness that were *feeding* illnesses.

This is what was happening when Jesus challenged the man who'd lingered by the Bethesda pool for thirty-eight years to get up off the mat and accept responsibility for his wellbeing. The men who were aiming to stone the woman caught in adultery to consider their *own* sins first. Society as a whole to see women and children differently. Simon-the-Pharisee to embrace the reconciling power of love. The sophisticated and powerful to drop 'empire' thinking with its assumptions and prejudices and become like little children again. His closest disciples to value service flowing from love as the real measure of greatness rather than power and position.

Benjamin remembered an adage that captured the spirit of this lesson: each person has two bears inside—a good bear and an evil bear. The bear that prevails is the one you feed.

Preaching to heal asks those who are ill to quit feeding the evil bear who is causing the illness and to feed the good bear instead.

* * * *

Lesson Four: Trust God.

Slowly Benjamin realized that although preachers can *offer* healing, they are not in control—no more than Jesus was.

Jesus demonstrated that preachers could have an unreproachable prayer life. They could habitually meet people where they are and offer alternatives to illness in the most compelling way possible, but ultimately, they had no control over the outcome. They could not coerce, force, or manipulate others to bring healing about.

Preaching to heal is a ministry of trusting God.

For the first time, Benjamin noticed how open-ended the Gospel stories are. We know what healing Jesus offered and whether it was initially accepted or rejected. But (for the most part), we do not know what happened after the story ended.

Did the woman who was about to be stoned sin no more? Was the person who was saved by the Good Samaritan changed by the healing love of an enemy? Did Gestus, the unrepentant thief on the wrong side of the cross, have a change of heart before he breathed his last? Did the rich young man change his mind, sell his stuff, and follow Jesus? And what happened when Lazarus's physical life finally ended?

He recalled Sophia's words that it's easier to love God than it is to trust God. In his heart he knew they were true. Benjamin knew he wanted to be in charge. He wanted a checklist that ensured everything would turn out according to his plans. But, as the Gospels demonstrate, he saw he was not going to get it.

Sophia had told him, "In the face of suffering that confuses and confounds us, it can be a struggle to remember that we do not heal on our own. We are conduits of the healing power of God—absolute, mysterious love that defies our comprehension even as we do our utmost to connect others to it.

"With neither control nor understanding, we are left to trust God, who created humans with the ability to choose great good or unspeakable evil. We are left to trust God, whose creation exists in time and space where the only certainty is physical death. We are left to trust God, who permits uncertainty and indeterminacy as the price of free will and allows pain to pave a path to authentic love," she added.

* * * *

Lesson Five: Disciplined discipleship promotes healing

Jesus modeled the practices of prayer, meeting people where they are, funding a new imagination, and trusting God. But every bit as necessary, Benjamin realized, Jesus umbrellaed these practices with *disciplined discipleship*. The Gospels reflect his unwavering commitment to bring God's healing love to the world with every word and deed. *This* discipline—*this* steadfast control over desires, impulses, and emotions for the sake of bringing healing to the world—was the path Jesus invited his contemporary and future disciples to embrace.

Jesus's example is not an easy path to follow. Indeed, the Gospels are a chronicle of challenges every disciple can expect to face: times when we are tempted by the lure of possessions, prestige, and power (just as Jesus faced them in the desert during his forty days of testing). Times of frustration when we must confront unthinking "moneychangers" who have lost sight of our *real* mission, just as Jesus confronted them outside of the Temple. Times of loss when grief so overcomes us that it is impossible not to weep, just as Jesus wept by Lazarus's tomb. Times of darkness when our prayer seems to be falling on deaf ears, like Jesus when he sweated blood in the Garden of Gethsemane. Times when we must muster great courage to be faithful to our call, just as Jesus did every time he spoke a truth that went against culture's grain. Times of rejection and betrayal, when those we believe will be with us fall asleep on the job.

Responding with grace and love doesn't just happen. Jesus's model of preaching to heal is *such* a radical way of living that it requires extraordinary self-discipline to stay the course.

* * * *

"I don't know whether I have the strength to be that disciplined," Benjamin had admitted to Sophia at the end of their conversation, recalling the downward spiral of darkness and doubt that brought him to the farm in the first place.

"You *don't* have the strength on your own," Sophia agreed. "No one does. The discipline to follow Jesus—to remain steadfast to a life of preaching that heals—comes from grace. *God* gives us the strength; we respond with a life of discipline: *intentionality*."

"Intentionality," Benjamin repeated thoughtfully.

"Our second pylon for preaching that heals," Sophia replied.

— Chapter 6 —

Pylon Two: 'Intentional'

A Path to Interiority for Preaching that Heals

I.

When Sophia arrived at the farmhouse near noon, she found Benjamin seated at a picnic table on the patio deep in thought. He'd spent the morning summarizing five Gospel lessons for preaching that heals on an index card he planned to keep in his Bible:

1. Prayer is the conduit of healing.
2. Meet people where they are.
3. Fund a new imagination.
4. Trust God.
5. Disciplined discipleship promotes healing.

Although he was satisfied with what he'd written, Benjamin was struck by how difficult it would be to *practice* these lessons consistently.

Benjamin *knew* he was disciplined. In fact, he couldn't imagine being a Catholic priest or a minister in any denomination *without* discipline. It seemed almost every waking moment was scheduled for him: prescribed prayer, sacramental celebrations, teaching, visits to the hospital and the homebound, and *constant* meetings. Then add emergency calls, weddings, funerals, and counseling appointments to an already-full schedule. Benjamin was *supposed* to take Sunday afternoons and Mondays off, but he seldom did.

Although he'd been energized by his conversations with Sophia, Benjamin had to admit he now felt swallowed by a wave of discouragement. As he thought about his own situation, it was clear that more than discipline was needed for preaching that heals.

* * * *

Noticing Benjamin's angst, Sophia gently asked, "What's going on?"

"Maybe I'm too caught up in a 'ministry-by-checklist' mentality," Benjamin began, "but when I think about the schedule I'm already keeping, I don't know how much *more* disciplined—how much *more* intentional—I can be."

"You've realized something significant," Sophia reassured him, "and you are right. You can be *perfectly* disciplined. You can be *absolutely* intentional. Yet you can *still* find yourself stuck in the dark abyss that separates *head* and *heart*, making healing virtually impossible.

"We will call that dark abyss *collective consciousness*," she added.

"*Collective consciousness?*" Benjamin scrunched his nose. "I feel we've just entered the Twilight Zone."

"In some ways, we *have*," Sophia laughed. "Collective consciousness is the 'group-think' that locks us into conformity. We find ourselves following the lead of others . . . looking at the world through someone else's glasses rather than trying to see as God wants us to see.

"Because collective consciousness is the insidious cause of every avoidable illness on earth, it's important to understand it," she added.

II.

Continuing, Sophia asked, "Benjamin, have you ever considered that *your* spirituality (the basis for how you think and choose) is influenced by *more* than your life experiences? It's shaped by the people closest to you, where you live, your education, your vocation, your religion, the groups to which you belong, and so much more.

"For example, tell me about the shirt you are wearing," she challenged.

He looked down at his well-worn Chicago Cubs T-shirt. "I've had this for ages."

"But why *this* team?" Sophia asked.

In spite of himself, Benjamin chuckled, "You sound like many people I know!"

Becoming serious, he reflected, "Well, I've *always* liked the Cubs. My parents—my whole family—are fans. I grew up watching them on TV, and once or twice a year, we'd take the train to Chicago to catch a game. Half the people I know are Cubs fans and the other half like the St. Louis Cardinals. It's a friendly rivalry . . . something to talk about."

"A fun example of collective consciousness!" Sophia said. "Your parents—your family—always watched the Cubs. You watched with them and enjoyed going to their games. You learned about your team's members and their rivals. It's just part of your life.

"But what about forms of collective consciousness that *aren't* so innocent and harmless? Accepting racism and sexism without thinking. Judging people by how much money they make or how powerful they are. Accepting abuse as a normal part of life. Believing we have no responsibility for the environment. Thinking that the only life worth living is an independent life that relies on no one else. Assuming we can't change bad situations, so why bother to try?

"These attitudes can be so deeply entrenched that we may not even be aware of them," Sophia added. "Left unchallenged, they *do* cause illness. They *do* infest the world."

* * * *

Benjamin recalled, "I remember you telling me how Pope Francis shocked the world—started a 'quiet revolution'—just by acting in a Christ-like manner during his earliest days as pope. He refused to get caught up in the trappings of careerism, power, and wealth that had seeped into the church, and he challenged those who were."

Sophia nodded. "Our shock at his Christ-like actions proves how easy it is to be *lured* into collective consciousness. Pope Francis challenged patterns of thinking and choosing that had blinded us to glaring inconsistencies between Jesus's teaching and the world around us," she said.

"Hans Christian Andersen captured the blinding lull of collective consciousness in his fairy tale, *The Emperor's New Clothes*. Do you remember the story, Benjamin?"

He nodded. "Everyone was complimenting the ruler on his fine clothing until a young child yelled out, 'The emperor doesn't have any clothes on!'"

Benjamin became quiet. "It took a *child* to see it. Could this be what Jesus meant when he said, 'Unless you become like a little child, you will not enter heaven' (Matt 18:3)?"

"Yes, and it's a big *unless*," Sophia said. "*Unless* we learn to see past collective consciousness that blinds us to the truth. *Unless* we learn to live beyond the inevitability that separates *head* from *heart* and keeps us locked into the abyss of all illness. *Unless* we take ownership of our souls through *self-appropriation*."

"But how can we *know* whether we are owning our souls?" Benjamin asked.

"We can make Interiority Analysis a habit," Sophia replied.

"Interiority Analysis?" Benjamin asked.

"Interiority Analysis," Sophia affirmed. "It's a method that can be learned and, once learned and practiced, equips us to recognize and respond to illnesses caused by collective consciousness. It is essential for preaching that heals.

"Are you interested in learning this method, Benjamin?" she asked.

"I am," he replied.

III.

"We'll start with the rationale." Sophia began. "Interiority Analysis was introduced in 1957 by a Jesuit priest, Bernard J. F. Lonergan, with his book, *Insight: A Study of Human Understanding*.[1] Lonergan describes how a human can stop living an unreflective, fearful life by learning how his or her own consciousness operates and becoming accountable for it."

"Human consciousness: the same thing as the human spirit, the seat of thinking and choosing," Benjamin recalled.

"The seat of thinking and choosing," Sophia stressed.

"How does Interiority Analysis work?" Benjamin asked.

"Interiority Analysis 'works' by teaching us how to use the scientific method to observe our spiritual operations of thinking and choosing *even as they are occurring*," Sophia replied. "With practice and over time, we can become adept at recognizing when our thought processes are flawed or when we are missing, ignoring, or overlooking important information in our decision-making. We can become adept at recognizing illnesses that are keeping us locked into the abyss. We can also begin to anticipate long-term consequences of actions and behaviors that will cause illness, depriving others (or any part of creation) of wellbeing."

"It sounds like a way to develop a conscience," Benjamin reflected.

"It is," Sophia replied.

---

1. Lonergan, *Insight*, xvii.

* * * *

"It is important to know that Interiority Analysis works within the triple-composite human anthropology we discussed yesterday," Sophia began. "Would you like a quick review?"

"Let me see if I've got this," Benjamin interjected. "The Organism, Psyche, and Spirit form the triple-composite 'whole,' working together *continuously* and *synchronously*. The Organism and Psyche form the body, and the Psyche and Spirit form the soul.

"In many ways, the Psyche is our connection to God. It provides the energy that fuels us throughout life in time and space. The body is the physicality that makes us recognizable as unique human beings. It interacts with the world through the five senses, accumulating memories that are stored in the Psyche. These memories enable us to form images, imagine, fantasize and dream. They also influence the Spirit (or consciousness), where thinking and choosing occur. The emotions—energy motors in the Psyche—are like Emergency Alert Systems that fire off without warning, alerting us to illness or wellbeing."

"You've got it!" Sophia exclaimed.

IV.

"Now, the method,"[2] she said.

"Within the triple-composite human, Interiority Analysis begins with the first step (or 'level' as Lonergan calls it): the *experience* of becoming aware of something new.[3] This new awareness can come from *anything*—the person's interactions with the world, memories that suddenly surface, emotions that fire up, images, dreams, fantasies, new ideas or insights, and—as the person's relationship with God grows—increasing sensitivity to proddings of the Holy Spirit.

---

2. Streeter, *Foundations of Spirituality*, 61–65.
3. Lonergan, *Insight*, xviii.

PYLON TWO: 'INTENTIONAL'

"But whatever the source, something enters your consciousness that wasn't there before," Sophia explained.

"I've had this experience," Benjamin reflected.

"I know you have," Sophia said gently. "One such experience was the awareness of your parishioner's scowl that caused you to doubt whether God wanted you to preach. The more we pay attention to what is happening, the more sensitized we become to illnesses that surround us and opportunities to offer healing, *even by our preaching*.

"Our challenge—our *imperative*—is to be attentive to the experience of new awareness," Sophia continued. "Obviously, we cannot heal illnesses that we fail to recognize. You should know that new awareness is *always* an invitation to live into greater love—with self, others, God, or any part of creation. It's *always* an opportunity to strengthen the *head*-to-*heart* connection. And, it's *always* a challenge to the collective consciousness and a call to change—something that causes many to ignore it."

* * * *

"Once we acknowledge the new awareness that has entered our consciousness, the second step (or 'level') of Interiority Analysis is to understand what we have experienced," Sophia said.

"The path to understanding will depend on what we have experienced, and most assuredly, it will require drawing on others' input. It may require research or conversations with others—whatever we need to develop informed ideas.

"Our imperative at this level is to be intelligent. Although this sounds simple enough, being intelligent will probably be one of the greatest challenges we face. It may push us far beyond our comfort zones and force us to reach out to people at (or beyond) our normal fringe of awareness. It may drive us to look into painful realities we have overlooked in the past and face uncomfortable truths that make us cringe. It will force us to look beyond personal agendas and long-held opinions, often shaking us to the core."

Benjamin looked up from the note he was writing. "It just occurred to me that we cannot look at illness without considering the part we've played in it."

"You are right," Sophia said, "but can you say more about this?"

Cringing a bit, he said, "Last year I worked with a group of eighth-graders, preparing them for Confirmation. I'd often take pizza to our get-togethers, which were around the time of the evening meal. One kid in the group always pushed to the front of the line, grabbing as much pizza as he could fit on his plate without regard for his classmates. I thought about saying something to him, but something inside caused me to resist.

"Later, I learned his story. He was the son of a single mom who worked evenings at a minimum-wage job without benefits. There was never much food in the house—certainly not enough for a growing teenager. It occurred to me that the problem was more than a starving teen. My student was a casualty of a far greater social justice issue. I began to learn as much as I could about the plight of the working poor and single mothers.

"The experience shook me up because I realized how easy it was for me to assume the worst about people—even kids—and to jump to conclusions without knowing anything . . . and without making any effort to understand," Benjamin added. "Here I am: a minister. And yet it is so easy to think in clichés that have nothing to do with living into love."

Looking at Benjamin, Sophia smiled, "The second level of Interiority Analysis: understanding."

* * * *

"We move on to the next—the third—level: judging," Sophia continued. "At this point, we scrutinize the various ideas that have surfaced from our attempt to understand what we've experienced.

"Consider your student, Benjamin. What ideas could you have formed from his behavior?"

PYLON TWO: 'INTENTIONAL'

Benjamin replied, "Without any attempt to understand, I could judge him to be greedy and selfish (which is what I did at first).

"Or I could look at the reasons for his behavior: not enough food because his single parent, despite her best efforts, simply could not afford to provide more. I could consider how impossible it would be to live on minimum wage, without benefits. I also could look into how many working poor there are in my community.

"In light of what I discovered about my own complicity, I could also judge that I was mired in a way of thinking that—with any heartfelt *thought* and in light of the Gospels, I wouldn't choose. Exactly what I *finally* realized I was doing," he admitted.

"Good!" Sophia said. "As you've just seen, judging involves evaluating the ideas we have formed in our attempt to understand. In the process, we will also need to judge our part in the illness, even if our part is complicity. Our challenge is to be reasonable. Do we have all of the information we need to make a sound judgment? Or is something missing?

"*If* we determine something is missing, being reasonable means taking a step back until we have all of the information we need to make a sound judgment. (By the way, this stepping back will be necessary any time vital new information surfaces.)

"Our goal in judging is to determine the most complete and truthful picture—to reach a place of internal *knowing*," Sophia added.

* * * *

"Up to this point, Interiority Analysis has focused on *thinking*, the intellect," Sophia continued. "At the fourth and final level, Interiority Analysis moves from thinking to *choosing*, the will. We decide whether or how to act in light of what we have come to know. Our challenge is to be responsible. This is especially important because, at this level, *conscience* emerges."

Benjamin interjected, "I'm seeing a potential problem here."

"What is it?" Sophia asked.

Benjamin replied, "Our decisions—our *conscience*—will only be as good as the thinking processes that support them."

"Too true!" Sophia exclaimed. "If we've short-changed the thinking processes, our decisions will reflect it. And we may cause or perpetuate illnesses unintentionally."

"What are some ways we can short-change thinking?" Benjamin asked.

"By ignoring red flags, settling for incomplete information, failing to ask questions that make us uncomfortable, or allowing our thinking to be influenced by fear or collective consciousness," Sophia replied.

* * * *

"Before we move on, there is one last part of Interiority Analysis— one that's so important that it umbrellas every level," Sophia said. "And that imperative is to be in love."[4]

"To be in love . . ." Benjamin repeated. "The umbrella . . ."

Sophia sat silently, giving him time to absorb the words.

"Being in love: it's the ultimate message and invitation in the Gospels," Benjamin reflected. "It's who Jesus is . . . the Word and the expression of love—*God*."

"It is," Sophia agreed. "It's such consuming, compassionate love that you can feel it in the gut. The Greek word for this love, 'splagchnizomai,' appears twelve times in the Gospel."

"'Splagchnizomai,'" Benjamin mused. "The gut-level love we are to feel as we experience, understand, judge, and decide."

"The overarching gut-level love," Sophia affirmed.

---

4. Streeter, *Foundations of Spirituality*, 70.

PYLON TWO: 'INTENTIONAL'

INTERIORITY ANALYSIS:
A Method for Self-Appropriation

V.

"Earlier this week, you mentioned that all sin originates in the human spirit, not in the body as many people believe," Benjamin recalled. "As we talk, it's becoming easier to see why."

"Exactly," Sophia agreed. "The body carries out what the Spirit decides, for better or worse. In fact, Lonergan identifies four biases that cause every human-inflicted (and therefore, avoidable) illness."

"Biases?" Benjamin asked.

"Biases: the intellectual blindness that hardens us to unwanted information," Sophia said. "The four types are *dramatic* bias, *individual* and *group* bias, and *general* bias.[5] Although this may sound confusing, I'm sure you've already encountered all four types.

"Let's begin with dramatic bias. You see it in people who have suffered personal trauma. Often this trauma is so severe that an afflicted person suppresses all memories of it. Yet, even if the memories are suppressed, the trauma afflicts the person. If the trauma goes unrecognized, healing is impossible."

Benjamin recalled, "A couple parishioners have told me that their addictions are an attempt to forget what has happened to them."

"Tragically, this is true," Sophia said. "Not just addictions, but other behavioral illnesses—anxiety, eating disorders, cutting, and depression among them—are often the result of dramatic bias. People who have been severely traumatized may try to block their pain through 'self-medication' with substances. They may be so numb that they just want to feel something. Or they may live in a constant state of anxiety or depression."

Benjamin shook his head. "Dramatic bias doesn't sound like something I—or *any* preacher—can heal by preaching."

"Probably not, but you still need to be aware of it and you can make others aware of it," Sophia agreed. "While prayer *can* and *does* heal dramatic bias, most victims also need therapy to unlock and deal with traumatic memories they have suppressed.

"Although we can help our parishioners become aware of dramatic bias, preaching more readily provides healing for the other types of bias," she added.

---

5. Streeter, *Foundations of Spirituality*, 67–70.

PYLON TWO: 'INTENTIONAL'

* * * *

"The other biases are related to thinking," Sophia continued, "and they can be deadly. Let's start with *individual* and *group* biases. This bias is prejudice and close-mindedness that limits our ability to question for truth. Can you think of examples, Benjamin?"

"Easily," he said. "Sexism. Racism. Religious hatred. Gay-bashing. Looking down at the poor as lazy and lacking a work ethic. The list is endless."

"It *is* endless," Sophia agreed, "and it's not harmless. Individual and group biases categorize, label, and marginalize unknown others based on habits that have nothing to do with love and truth. In extreme cases, they can even lead to murder. Think about genocides and terrorism as examples. It's especially horrifying that these biases are so deep-seated they often escape our notice.

"The result is the fear- or hate-laden diminishment of others. We see it in attitudes and institutions that deny women, the chronically ill, the aged, people of color, and others the opportunity to live to their fullest potential in the way they are called by God. We see it in hate-mongers who gather menacingly outside of churches that serve LGBTQ individuals. In schools where economically-disadvantaged students are given less consideration than their better-off classmates. In politics where immigrants of certain religions or nationalities are suspected of being terrorists, and more," Sophia added.

"The rotten fruit of group-think . . ." Benjamin reflected.

* * * *

"Lonergan's final bias is *general* or *theoretic*," Sophia continued. "This bias is what we might call 'anti-intellectualism.' It is pragmatic thinking that refuses to consider new discoveries and breakthroughs that threaten long-held beliefs or practices that have led to selfish, short-term gains.

"Can you think of an example of general bias, Benjamin?" she asked.

He thought for a minute. "This one is harder," he ventured, "but would an example be a politician who refuses to consider scientific evidence that attributes as many as 300-thousand deaths a year to global warming[6]? Or the doctor trained in Western biomedicine who refuses to learn about promising alternative treatments?"

"These are great examples!" Sophia exclaimed. "As you can see, general bias shuts down creative envisioning—the ability to 'fund' a new imagination—that is essential for preaching that heals. It locks us into illness, even in the face of new evidence and remedies."

VI.

"Once again, we have covered a great deal," Sophia said, "and you've taken some notes as we've talked. Would you like to review them?"

"I would," Benjamin began, reading from the index card he'd covered on both sides:

1. Intentionality fosters preaching that heals.
2. Living on auto-pilot is not intentionality.
3. Collective consciousness leads to conformity; undermines intentionality.
4. Self-appropriation overcomes collective consciousness
5. Interiority Analysis leads to self-appropriation.
6. Biases cause *all* avoidable illnesses.
7. Preaching that heals is *being in love*.

"A great summary," Sophia said.

"But I'm realizing something," Benjamin ventured. "That's how much illness and healing are tied to others. Preaching cannot heal on its own. Others must cooperate."

6. Vidal, "Global warming causes 300,000 deaths a year," May 29, 2009, the guardian.com.

PYLON TWO: 'INTENTIONAL'

"And that brings us to our next topic, our third pylon: holography, the relationality and science of preaching that heals," Sophia said.

"Let's meet at 9 tomorrow morning at Presence Point to continue."

— Interlude —

Reflection on Creation's Interrelatedness

Presence Point was the name given to a clearing in the pine forest that overlooked a shallow ravine. For Benjamin, it was impossible not to feel the presence of God at this sacred place.

He arrived at the overlook early. Taking a seat on one of the two old concrete-based bus-stop benches that had been positioned to form a gentle letter "V" a safe distance from the drop-off, Benjamin poured a cup of coffee from his thermos and inhaled the pine-scented air. For years, he had come to Presence Point to read and to pray. Somehow, it was easier to find answers here—to grasp elusive truths, assuage doubts, and discern the will of God.

Benjamin recalled the day at this very spot when he first understood that God had created a cosmos that was continually changing. As he observed leaves falling from autumn trees, he'd grasped that instant-to-instant change was divinely ordained.

On this particular morning, Benjamin especially noticed the sun glistening on the creek at the floor of the ravine below. It was the type of creek that scientists call "meandering": instead of flowing downhill in a more-or-less straight line, this creek snaked from side to side.

Over time, Benjamin knew, the course of the creek would change. Some changes would be nearly imperceptible from season to season—for example, those caused by the flow of water carrying loose sediment and rock from one place to another. Other changes would be sudden, caused by violent wind and storms that toppled

INTERLUDE: REFLECTION ON CREATION'S INTERRELATEDNESS

dying trees or eroded the hillside, interrupting the water's path. All would make their mark.

As he observed the world around him, Benjamin knew that for better or worse, in God's creation—where All is connected to All—nothing could ever stay the same.

— Chapter 7 —

Pylon Three: 'Holographic'

The Vision and Science of Preaching that Heals

I.

Sophia had barely taken her seat on the bench next to Benjamin's before he began to talk.

"I've been watching the creek and thinking about how it's affected by *everything*," he blurted out. "Falling branches . . . otters building their dams . . . loose rocks and sediment on the creek bed, moved by the sheer force of water . . . run-off from nitrogen-based fertilizers used by the farmer down the road. *Everything* matters."

"You're so right!" Sophia exclaimed. "We live in an interrelated world. *Everything* and *everyone* impact the wellbeing of *everything* and *everyone* to an extent we've only begun to grasp in the past century."

"Through science?" Benjamin mused.

"Through science," Sophia affirmed. "Scientific breakthroughs not only give us insight into God's creation, but they also give us new and exciting clues about how God intends us to live and preach. Let me share some breathtaking examples, Benjamin:

"In only a century, we've learned that *every* part of creation—from the smallest particle to the most reflective human—evolved from a single creation event attributable to an Uncreated Cause (God!) some 13.8 billion years ago.[1]

---

1. Swimme and Tucker, *Journey of the Universe*, 6.

PYLON THREE: 'HOLOGRAPHIC'

"We've learned that while creation began with massive inflation that has carried matter apart for billions of years, this inflation is countered by *attraction* (gravity), which brings two entities together with each sacrificing *something* to become a greater whole.[2]

"We've learned that evolution *always* leads to greater consciousness (awareness of the other) and complexity (sacrificial bonds that result from this awareness), with more complex beings 'nested' in what has come before.[3]

"We've learned that interrelatedness (called 'entanglement' in physics) exists to a once-unthinkable extent—that two particles with only the briefest contact will *continue* to influence each other after the contact, *even at a distance*.[4]

"And we've learned that *thought* (including prayer) can cause change, again, *even at a distance*,"[5] Sophia added. "This is *not* weird science, Benjamin. It's God's creation, countering the tendency to pull apart with attraction to communion 'so that all may be one (John 17:21).'"

Benjamin said thoughtfully, "These discoveries give new depth to Jesus's words, 'Whatever you did for one of these least of mine, you did to me' (Matt 25:40)."

"They *do*," Sophia said, "and this meaning should reach into every part of our lives. To forget our sacred connection is to perpetuate illness rather than God's healing love."

II.

"I observed you when you realized that although preachers can *offer* healing, they cannot make it *happen*," Sophia continued. "As you grasped this truth, you looked like you'd been struck by lightning. You were positively *charged*!

---

2. Swimme and Tucker, *Journey of the Universe*, 8.
3. Cannato, *Radical Amazement*, 98.
4. Russell, *Quantum Shift*, 60–61.
5. Russell, *Quantum Shift*, 59.

"The idea is so basic, but it's never hit me until *now*," Benjamin's voice trailed off.

"Don't beat up on yourself for not realizing it sooner," Sophia said. "You are not alone. Our seemingly sophisticated Western culture has lost sight of the absolute relationality of creation. It truly *is* more than holistic; it's *holographic*. *Every* part is inextricably linked, influencing and being influenced by *every other part*.

"A holographic vision of creation is essential for preachers who want to heal *even by their preaching*, because, without it, we lack the graced imagination to see the full grip of illness and its effect on others.

"It is so important that it's the third pylon of preaching that heals," she added

* * * *

"But why is it so difficult to acknowledge our interrelatedness?" Benjamin asked.

"That's a question German philosopher Karl Theodor Jaspers attempted to answer in 1949," Sophia began. "Jaspers recognized that a notable shift in the overarching cosmic consciousness occurred between three and two millennia ago, beginning somewhere around 900 and 800 B.C.E. and continuing until around 200 B.C.E. Jaspers called this period the 'Axial Age.'[6]

"During this time, the consciousness of our earliest ancestors—which had been communal, deeply connected to nature, and focused on appeasing the gods (or, in the case of our Judeo-Christian forbearers, *God*) slowly gave way to a consciousness of control, autonomy, and individuality. Humans began to understand they could take charge of many forces of nature, to believe in the moral culpability of individuals as well as communities,[7] and to assume that humans had the right to *dominate* the rest of creation for their own purposes," she added.

---

6. See Delio, *Making All Thinks New*; Streeter; *Foundations of Spirituality*; and Institute for the Study of Human Knowledge, http://www.ishk.net.

7. Streeter, *Foundations of Spirituality*, 3–5.

PYLON THREE: 'HOLOGRAPHIC'

Benjamin sat quietly, absorbing the idea before speaking. "You say that humans claimed *domination* over creation . . ."

"To *dominate* is to take total control over the other by whatever means are deemed necessary—including coercion, force, or manipulation, often with no or little consideration for the long-term consequences or the effect on others," Sophia said. "Domination stands in sharp contrast to the *dominion* God entrusted to humans in Genesis 1:28. Dominion is taking care of the other and working for the mutual benefit and greatest good for all."

"Domination versus dominion: a huge difference," Benjamin sighed.

* * * *

As a nature lover, Benjamin had been enthralled by Pope Francis's 2015 encyclical, *Laudato Si': On Care for Our Common Home*. He mentioned this to Sophia, adding, "I'm wondering if it's Pope Francis's holographic vision that gives *Laudato Si'* its depth and power?"

"Can you say more about this?" Sophia invited.

"Well," he began, "I've always agreed that this work (which many critics have derided as a tree-hugger's fantasy) is more about disordered human relationships than environmental devastation. It's about unregulated human greed and the willingness to exploit nature and other people for selfish reasons. I think Pope Francis hits the nail on the head when he says that *human* ecology must come first. For example, he writes about how poverty and the lack of steady work contribute to crises like climate change and how unmitigated greed pollutes our water supplies. Without human transformation and a willingness to come together for the greater good, nothing will change.

"I think seeing this way is what you mean by holographic vision," he finished.

"A good analysis, Benjamin," Sophia said.

"Perhaps," he said, "but the real question is how we begin to heal illnesses that are right before our eyes?"

"Are you ready to take a look at the healing dynamic?" Sophia asked.

"I am," Benjamin said.

III.

"Healing *always* begins with one person who recognizes the meaning of illness and decides to respond to it," Sophia said. "It's *always* a process of spiritual transformation—a change in thinking and choosing that moves one person to greater love."

"Strengthening the *head*-to-*heart* connection," Benjamin mused.

"Strengthening the *head*-to-*heart* connection," Sophia echoed.

"In his powerful theory of spiritual transformation,[8] Korean theologian Yung Suk Kim describes the first awareness of illness as an *I am no-one* moment in a person's life," she continued. "This new awareness brings a sense of discombobulation, discomfort, and uneasiness—a loss of wellbeing. We find ourselves in a foreign place. Everything seems strange, and we feel alienated from ourselves, others, and God."

"I experienced this with preaching," Benjamin reflected. "It's a painful place to be."

"It *is* painful," Sophia acknowledged. "It's a time when we lose our footing, our certainty about how things are, and our place in the world—*our sense of self.*

"Kim writes that this loss can be caused by natural disasters or circumstances outside of our control, by knowledge of personal wrong-doing, or by a decision to sacrifice ourselves for others. But, as he stresses, *sometimes* it's caused by something we can't readily identify.[9]

"No matter what the cause, the question is: *what are we going to do?*" Sophia asked. "Are we going to dismiss the pain (Kim calls it 'the enemy')? Or engage it?"

---

8. Kim, *A Transformative Reading of the Bible*, 22–26.
9. Kim, *A Transformative Reading of the Bible*, 22.

PYLON THREE: 'HOLOGRAPHIC'

"This sounds a bit like Interiority Analysis," Benjamin observed.

"In some ways, it is," Sophia said. "All spiritual transformation begins with a new awareness of the illness, and all healing moves us from the familiar status quo. But Interiority Analysis is a *method* to be learned and practiced. What Kim is describing is a *dynamic* that draws us forward—or not (as we choose).

"In the strange uncertainty of the *I am no-one* moment, we become more open to each other and God. In psychological terms, it's a time when our super-ego dissolves,[10] and we die to ourselves a little more. Our encounter with illness enables us to see beyond the artificial lures of the world and turn to God, who is always calling us to greater love."

* * * *

Benjamin reflected, "'Unless a grain of wheat falls to the ground and dies, it remains just a grain of wheat; but if it dies, it bears much fruit' (John 12:24) . . ."

Nodding, Sophia said, "And so we emerge as new creations, capable of bearing more fruit in what Kim calls our new *I am some-one* moment. With our vitalized and more sensitized understanding, we can enter into Kim's third moment of being—*I am one-for-others*. Here, we recognize the pain of others because we have experienced it ourselves."

"I think I understand," Benjamin said. "The *I am no-one* moment is a time of dying to self and our expectations about life as we encounter illness in which we're playing a part, directly or indirectly. We recognize the need for healing, even though healing will challenge group norms and require change. We die to what has been and who we have been *because* the pain of staying where we are becomes greater than the discomfort and risk of change. We emerge from this 'death' with a new sense of *I am some-one* and—because of our experiences—are better able to relate to others in a new *I am one-for-others* sense."

10. Kim, *A Transformative Reading of the Bible*, 23.

* * * *

Nodding, Sophia added, "There's one other point Kim stresses—an important one. *This healing dynamic, this spiritual transformation, is not a smooth and linear process.* The *I am no-one* moment does not neatly lead to the *I am some-one* moment, and then to the *I am one-for-others* moment. All three modes continually work together, in tension,[11] pressing us to live into greater love—*if* we are willing to cooperate with grace."

Benjamin sat quietly, taking in the idea.

Finally, he said, "Let me see if I can explain this. The closer our relationship to God, the more sensitive we are to what is happening around us, and the better we can recognize illness. But healing is an ongoing process. We can reach a place of resolution in one area of life (at least for a time) yet still find ourselves challenged in other areas. This divine draw is always attracting us to greater love in a wider-reaching *holographic* way."

"Exactly," Sophia said. "Our lives in time and space really *are* a journey to greater love—to God, *if* we allow them to be."

"And so we have one person who is responding to grace—whose spirit is being transformed," Benjamin said. "Then what?"

"This person reaches out to others by preaching in word and deed," Sophia smiled. "But as you now know, Benjamin, our preaching cannot make healing happen. We can only begin the process. And this is where it is helpful to understand what might be called the *tentacles of illness* and the *trajectory of healing*."

IV.

"Have you ever thought about the *tentacles* of illness, Benjamin?" Sophia challenged.

"Do you mean the *reach* of illness and its impact on others?" he asked.

"Yes," she nodded.

---

11. Kim, *A Transformative Reading of the Bible*, 27.

PYLON THREE: 'HOLOGRAPHIC'

Pausing, Benjamin said, "A passage from Exodus comes to me. As God gave the first commandment to Moses, God said, 'For I, the Lord, your God am a jealous God, inflicting punishment for their father's wickedness on the children who hate me, down to the third and fourth generations; but bestowing mercy down to the thousandth generation, on the children of those who love me and keep my commandments (Exodus 20: 5b-6).'"

"What does this passage suggest to you, Benjamin?" Sophia asked.

"That the consequences of sin—*illness*—extend far beyond the sinner, long after the sin," he said. "Sin has an energy and a memory of its own. It carries on, entrapping people who were not directly involved in its poison web. I've seen this in many broken families."

"And what does the passage say to you about the nature of sin?" Sophia pressed.

"Well, it occurs to me *now* that the words 'hate' and 'love' are *relationship* words," Benjamin reflected. "'Hate' implies a break in the relationship with God—the *head*-to-*heart* connection—that enables us to do something that hurts others. 'Love,' on the other hand—God's will for us—promotes ongoing wellbeing and peace by serving the greater good."

"And the commandments themselves?" Sophia challenged.

"I see their relationality—their *holographic vision*," Benjamin reflected.

* * * *

"Healing, then, is a process of reconciliation that seeks to restore broken relationships," Sophia said. "The *preacher-healer* (*any* person who confronts illness in word and deed for the greater glory of God) makes the illness known to others who may not even recognize it. Like any folk healer, the preacher confronts the symptoms of the illness and challenges both the afflicted *and* the afflicting, inviting them to embrace a new reality.

"In Christian preaching, this new reality—this new imagination that replaces illness with wellbeing—flows from the Gospels," she added. "Healing words are addressed to a particular community, at a particular time, in the name of greater communal love."

Benjamin thought for a moment. "So, my aim—and the aim of every *pulpit* preacher—is to share God's healing love in a way that inspires others *to actualize* this love in the world. The fruit of this love is a greater awareness and willingness to consider the 'other'—a communion of greater consciousness and complexity."

"Yes," Sophia said. "Inspiring those we serve to become Christ to the other.'"

V.

The Trajectory of Healing

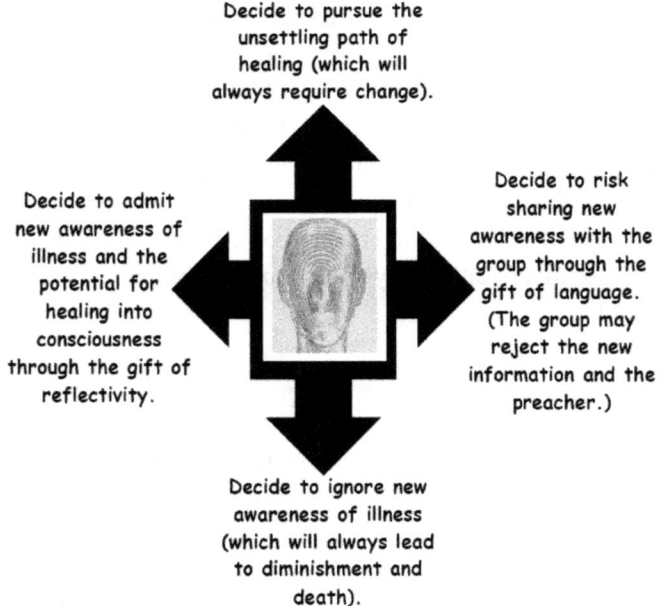

Decide to pursue the unsettling path of healing (which will always require change).

Decide to admit new awareness of illness and the potential for healing into consciousness through the gift of reflectivity.

Decide to risk sharing new awareness with the group through the gift of language. (The group may reject the new information and the preacher.)

Decide to ignore new awareness of illness (which will always lead to diminishment and death).

My adaptation of Judy Cannato's diagram of the dilemma of change in *Radical Amazement*.

PYLON THREE: 'HOLOGRAPHIC'

"But what about the *trajectory of healing*?" Benjamin asked.

"We can literally draw a picture to illustrate this point," Sophia began. "The picture I am going to share is based on the work of a brilliant theologian, Judy Cannato, and is derived from her book, *Radical Amazement: Contemplative Lessons from Black Holes, Supernovas, and Other Wonders of the Universe*.[12]

"One person is at the center of a diamond-shaped diagram that resembles an upright cross," Sophia began. "The person at the center who is confronting illness and the need for healing is pulled by two separate pairs of tension.

"On the horizontal axis, the person experiences tension between new awareness of illness and his or her standing in a larger group. Preaching to heal is always a risky business that challenges group norms and the status quo. The larger group may resist the call to healing, reject the person who dares to preach it, and even break up because of it.

"On the vertical axis, the person faces a tension between a lower desire to ignore the illness and try to stay the same (a decision that will always lead to diminishment, dissolution, and death) and a higher draw to healing and transcendence (which will always require change and will always lead to greater communion and love).

"But the choice is always left to the person because God has given us free will," she added. "We can entomb ourselves by ignoring illness or respond and rise above it."

* * * *

"So, the person in the center decides to share his or her new awareness of illness and challenge the group to healing . . ." Benjamin said.

"Based on our conversation, what do you think happens next?" Sophia asked.

Benjamin considered the question for several minutes. Finally, he ventured: "I think the group and each person in it will

---

12. Cannato, *Radical Amazement*, 98.

be challenged. Do we—*do I*—acknowledge the experience of new awareness that has entered our—*my*—consciousness? We—*I*—can try to dismiss the new awareness, but because it has already entered consciousness, we—*I*—will be unsuccessful."

"You bring up an interesting point," Sophia interjected. "Awareness always changes us, even if we resist it. It subtly impacts how we think and choose and—over time—may lead to healing even if we resist it at first. Please continue with what you think will happen if the offer of healing is accepted."

"If the vision of healing is accepted, it will require changing how we—*I*—think, choose, and act. Change is never easy, and, depending on the illness, it could radically alter how we—*I*—live. And, at some later time, it may compel us—*me*—to share what we—*I*—have come to know and offer healing to others," Benjamin finished.

"You begin to see the dilemma faced by every person who wishes to heal, *even by their preaching*," Sophia said gently.

* * * *

"Yikes," he sighed under his breath.

"Yikes is right," Sophia echoed, opening her backpack and handing him the drawing. "It's an appropriate reflection of the risky business of seeing holographically and healing, *even by our preaching.*

"We have one last pylon to go—*spoken*," Benjamin said, "and I leave tomorrow."

"Why don't we meet on the bridge at 7 tonight for our last conversation?" Sophia suggested.

Choked up in a way that caught him off guard, Benjamin simply said, "Thank you."

— Interlude —

Reflection on the Anxiety of Feeling Like Something Is Missing

There are few times as strange as the last afternoon on an away-from-home vacation. The 'here-but-not-yet' quality is suffocating. You would like to relax and feel the vacation-time release one last time before returning to the real world, but it is impossible. The transition and the return have already begun.

And so, it was.

Benjamin spent his last afternoon at the farm washing a few dishes, cleaning the kitchen, doing a little laundry, packing (if you could call it that: he'd hardly been styling at the farm), and preparing for an early departure the next morning. Although he'd made time for a hike, the focus and rhythm were different—distracted.

He knew the week had been powerful—transformational; he didn't know how what he had learned would translate as he returned to his official, ordained life. He wanted to revel in what he had absorbed. Instead, he was gripped with anxiety.

As he'd left Sophia earlier in the day, Benjamin had a lump in his throat. The lessons he'd thought he mastered during their conversations were still with him, but he wanted more time. He'd wanted to scream, "I am not ready yet! I do not know whether I can do what I know I need to do. I am not ready to let go and trust—not worthy of being a conduit of God's love."

Walking toward the unfinished bridge at a quarter to seven, he wondered whether all would ever be well.

— Chapter 8 —

Pylon Four: 'Spoken'

*Communication Principles for
Preaching that Heals*

I.

Sophia immediately noticed that Benjamin's mood and energy level had changed as he arrived at the bridge and slumped into the unoccupied Adirondack chair.

"You seem . . . *deflated*?" she observed quizzically.

"I am," he replied. "This week's been great, but the thought of going home tomorrow terrifies me. I know I've learned a lot and changed a lot. But I can't shake the awful feeling that something important is missing."

"Something *critical* is missing," Sophia affirmed, "and that's the fourth pylon of preaching that heals, *spoken*."

* * * *

"Until now, we've focused on the spiritual dimensions of preaching that heals—new ways of thinking and choosing. But at last, we've come to the point of *action*, where Word comes to light through words," Sophia said. "Our *spoken* words . . ."

"*Spoken*," Benjamin said, absorbing the word.

"Spoken," Sophia repeated. "In pulpit preaching, it's the definitive *verbal* act that gives visibility to the preacher's encounter with God on behalf of a community—*or not*."

PYLON FOUR: 'SPOKEN'

"It's the *or not* that I find terrifying," Benjamin admitted.

"For good reason," Sophia said. "A preacher can have a strong *head*-to-*heart* connection and a solid vision of the aim of preaching, a thorough understanding of illness and healing, a deep knowledge and love of Scriptures, an intentional and prayerful life rooted in interiority, and the steadfast courage of holographic vision yet *still* miss the mark at the pulpit."

"But *how*?!?" Benjamin insisted.

"By ignoring the principles of good communication," Sophia said.

* * * *

"*Ignore* them?!?" Benjamin guffawed. "I'm not sure I ever *learned* them!"

"You're not alone," Sophia said sadly. "Although communication skills are essential in every human endeavor and constitutive of what it means to be human, and although they've been studied at least since the time of Aristotle, relatively few people have ever learned them or are even aware of them today. Given their importance in preaching, we're going to focus on them during this—our last—conversation."

Benjamin looked dejected. "How can an hour possibly be enough time if they're *that* important?"

"An hour's plenty of time to get started," Sophia reassured him, "and you can continue to learn more at home if you choose. I think you'll find that the basic principles, combined with everything else we've covered this week, will give you the confidence you need to offer healing to those you serve, *even by your preaching*."

Catching his eye, she smiled. "Are you ready?"

"I am," Benjamin replied.

II.

Going into teaching mode, Sophia began: "*All* communication starts with a **Sender** who wants to share information (a **Message**) with another person or a group (the **Receiver**). Although we all know people who seem to talk just to hear themselves and pay little attention to what they are saying, let's assume *this* Sender (let's say the preacher) has a reason to send *this* particular Message (the sermon or homily) to *this* Receiver (the congregation). The Sender's first task is to figure out how to present (**Encode**) the Message.

"*How* the Sender encodes the Message not only will depend on the nature of the Message but also the way it will be delivered (the communication **Channel**). As you can imagine, the way you prepare (encode) a verbally-spoken homily will be quite different from how you prepare a text message or a sign for a display in a store.

"A Channel may be *direct* and *synchronous* (one person speaking to another person or a group face to face) or *indirect* and *asynchronous* (for example, digital or electronic media), but the Channel should *always* influence how the Sender encodes the Message."

* * * *

"*If* the Receiver is paying attention and decides to receive the message at all, the Receiver will **Decode** the message (interpret its meaning). In the best scenario, the Receiver will understand the Message *exactly* how the Sender intended and respond (offer **Feedback**) accordingly," Sophia finished, producing a diagram from her backpack:

Benjamin took the diagram and studied it briefly. "Okay, I think I get it," he said.

"I'm sure you do," Sophia said, "but keep in mind that this is an *ideal* communication model. In real life, communication is seldom so straightforward."

* * * *

Sophia took a bold marker and quickly transformed the simple model into a Venn diagram with one bracket around the **Sender/Encoder** and **Message/Channel** and another intersecting bracket around the **Message/Channel** and **Decoder/Receiver** half.

"Each set of brackets represents the communication environment for either the **Sender/Encoder** or the **Decoder/Receiver**," she explained.

"Communication environment?" Benjamin puzzled.

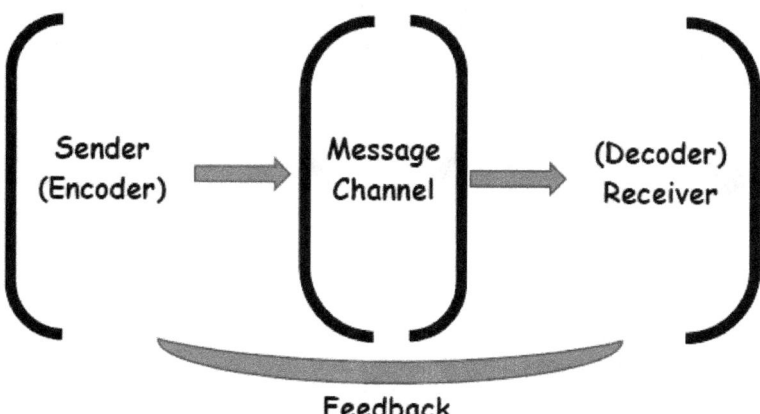

Feedback

"The sum of life experiences that influences how the Sender understands the Message and how the Receiver understands it," Sophia said. "The larger the intersection—in other words, the more the experiences of the **Sender** 'match' those of the **Receiver**—the more likely it is that effective (or any!) communication will occur."

"This has just gotten infinitely more complicated," Benjamin observed. "If I encode a message that the receiver *can't decode*—if there's no common ground, then I will fail to communicate at all . . ."

"Let alone offer healing through the spoken word," Sophia agreed.

* * * *

"There's one other thing we need to consider: **Noise**," Sophia said, picking up her marker and drawing bold, jagged vertical lightning bolts that severed the diagram on either side of the words **Message/Channel**.

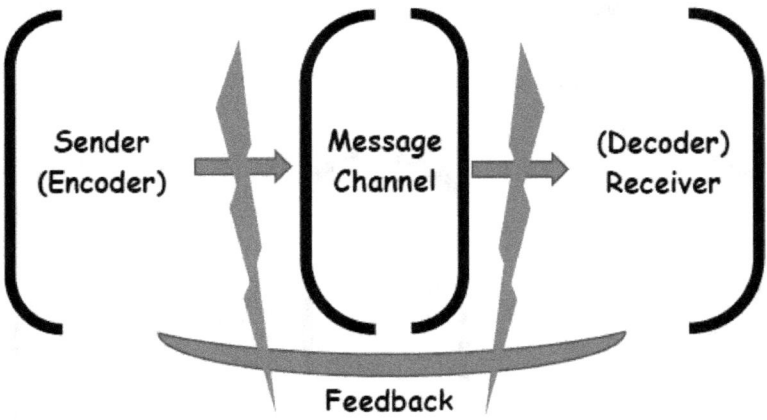

"Noise?" Benjamin groaned.

"Noise," Sophia echoed. "It's the bane of every preacher's existence—uncontrollable interference that keeps your Message from being received the way you intended (or at all).

"Noise can be *external*: think of the screaming child, the parishioner who faints, or the PA system that short-circuits in the middle of your sermon. Or it can be *internal*: the parishioner who is worrying about work or just had a knock-down/drag-out fight in the car with a teenager on the way to church. Regardless of the source, the result is the same. Noise diverts the Receiver's attention, muffles the Message (no matter how powerful the Message is), or altogether blocks it."

III.

"Now, let's make this personal, Benjamin," Sophia said. "I'd like you to remember a time when you were in a situation where you had no idea what was being communicated. Use your imagination to recall as many details as you can—what you saw, smelled, heard, tasted, touched, and how you *felt*."

Benjamin thought. "Once I wandered into a market in Vancouver's Chinatown. Everyone seemed to be native-born Chinese. They all spoke Chinese, and all the signs were in Chinese. The smells were different than any I'm used to—spicy, pungent. The displays startled me: unplucked ducks hanging from ceiling hooks and drawer-like display cases filled with webbed feet—a delicacy? I couldn't even recognize lots of stuff—foods, powders, various roots. But even when I *could* recognize some of the items—miniature houses and cars made from colorful tissue paper—I didn't understand them," his voice trailed off.

"And yet, every word, every sign, and every item had meaning and value to the customers. Displays were arranged with them in mind. The market owner (the Sender) probably spent a great deal of time and effort trying to understand and respond to the needs of the customers (the Receivers)," Sophia observed. "Sales depended on it."

"Yes, but it was all babble to me," Benjamin exclaimed. "*Totally* discombobulating!"

* * * *

"You used an interesting word—*babble*," Sophia observed. "Does it remind you of a story in Scripture?

"The Tower of Babel in Genesis, Chapter Eleven," Benjamin piped in.

Sophia nodded. "It's a myth about people who—because of their egotism and desire to be like God—lose their ability to communicate. Verbal language is no longer universal. Without a great deal of effort, people can't understand each other or be understood.

"Benjamin: *this is our story!*" she stressed. "Did you know that approximately 6,500 languages are spoken in the world today?"

"Which means that I can't understand most spoken words," Benjamin reflected.

"And this is only the beginning!" Sophia continued. "As you experienced in the Chinatown market, there are also cultural aspects, including *nonverbal* language. UCLA professor Albert Mehrabian discovered that *verbal* language accounts for only seven percent of communication. *Nonverbal* language accounts for the overwhelming ninety-three percent!"

"*Nonverbal* language?" Benjamin asked. "Body language and tone of voice?"

"Yes," Sophia replied. "Mehrabian found that body language accounts for fifty-five percent of what we communicate and tone of voice, thirty-eight percent. Together, body language and tone will reinforce what we're trying to say or totally obliterate it."

"I get tone of voice," Benjamin said, "but can you say more about body language?"

"Body language covers a wide gamut: posture, facial expression, eye contact, whether we lean into a conversation or pull away from it, the distance maintained between people, subtle shows of resistance like crossed arms or legs, gestures like nodding, and more," Sophia replied.

* * *

"Yikes," Benjamin said. "So, preaching isn't just the words we choose. It's the total package."

"The total package," Sophia stressed.

Pausing, she added, "Your experience in the Chinatown market is perfectly understandable. You were immersed in a culture you didn't understand and weren't prepared to encounter. But what's more disconcerting is how often we fail to communicate even when we *do* share a language and a culture. It's intriguing to think about how often we subject our parishioners to Chinatown-like experiences *even—especially—by our preaching.*"

"But I've never intended to," Benjamin said.

"Of course not—and just being aware of the basic principles of communication will help you tremendously," Sophia reassured him.

"I think I understand, but would you help me see how these principles apply to preaching?" Benjamin asked.

"I thought you'd never ask," Sophia replied.

IV.

"We'll look at three common scenarios," Sophia began. "And, as we look at each one, I want you to think about how *you* have experienced it personally, as a person in the pew."

"A person in the pew?" Benjamin protested. "But I'm the preacher."

"*Now* you are, but you haven't always been," Sophia said. "By entering into these scenarios, you'll be far more likely to avoid them." Gently, she reminded him, "Keep in mind that *all* healing begins with the experience of new awareness of illness . . ."

"Okay. Point well taken," he said.

"More importantly, we'll use a technique that you can use at home," she added.

Scenario #1: Hijacking the Homily/Usurping the Sermon

Sophia began: "Our first scenario: Have you ever experienced a preacher who becomes more important than the Good News, Benjamin?"

"I think I know what you mean. I think I've witnessed it, and I'm pretty sure I've *done* it," he said. "By 'becoming more important than the Good News,' you mean that the preacher's actions and tone of voice steal the show—right?"

"Right," Sophia said.

"Recently, I attended a weekday Mass that one of my former classmates was celebrating," Benjamin recalled. "I'd taken the day off, and we were planning to go hiking and hang out after Mass.

"From the moment he entered the sanctuary, it was clear that something was 'off.' When he approached the pulpit, it was like he was half asleep. His lack of energy became the focus—that's what held my attention. Instead of paying attention to the Gospel or his preaching, I just sat there, wondering what was wrong.

"I wasn't the only one. At the back of the church after Mass, parishioner after parishioner asked him if he was okay. He responded in a weak voice that he'd had a rough night at the hospital," Benjamin recalled.

* * * *

"A good example!" Sophia exclaimed. "What do you think was going on?"

"Well, my classmate really *was* tired, and he obviously had been affected by whatever happened at the hospital," Benjamin reflected, "but I think there was more. He seemed to want the congregation to acknowledge how self-sacrificing he was . . . the crosses he was willing to carry on their behalf. I hate to say this, but I think it was sort of an ego thing. A 'look at how much I'm suffering for you' thing."

"There's no question that your vocation is difficult," Sophia said, looking at Benjamin with compassion. "It's human to want to be appreciated—to want to *matter*, and I have no doubt that your classmate's ministry at the hospital *did* matter. But there's no room at the pulpit for ego gratification."

"But what if it creeps in unintentionally?" Benjamin asked. "I mean, we're only human, and there are times when we have to preach when we're sick or exhausted."

PYLON FOUR: 'SPOKEN'

"Not to sound uncaring, but this a challenge of the ministry," Sophia said. "Preaching is a sacred trust and call from God. Part of living into this trust and call is doing our best to let God's healing love shine through. Preachers are *conduits*, never the main attraction.

"Barring unusual circumstances, you can bet that if a parade of parishioners is asking you what's wrong after Mass or telling you about great home remedies and over-the-counter drugs, you need to get a grip on your nonverbal communication," she added.

Scenario #2: Ignoring the Intersection

"I'm not trying to put you on the spot, Benjamin, but didn't you tell me that you once preached for twenty minutes on an obscure theological tractate to a church full of first- through sixth-grade kids who couldn't wait to get outside for a water fight?" Sophia asked.

"Guilty as charged," Benjamin grimaced, "and it was a disaster. The kids were fidgety, and the adults were irritated."

"Tell me why you chose to preach on that tractate that day," Sophia asked.

"Believe it or not, it was entirely in good faith," Benjamin said. "It was the feast of the Sacred Heart, and I wanted to share something that had been profoundly meaningful to me. The idea that the tractate would be totally inappropriate for this Mass at the end of a week-long kids' summer camp didn't even cross my mind."

"I believe you," Sophia said, "and I think your mistake is one that many preachers make with the best of intentions. It's easy for people of privilege—actually, for *anyone*—to ignore the intersection and assume others are in the same place—that they share the same experiences."

"People of privilege?" Benjamin protested. "I don't think of myself that way."

"And yet, you are," Sophia replied. "Among other things, you've had eight years of education after high school. You're one of only about thirteen percent of the U.S. population with a master's degree. Media companies have always understood this, which is why newspapers and newscasts are intentionally targeted to a ninth-grade (or lower) level."

"I didn't know that," Benjamin said.

"Your education had a purpose and came with an obligation. It equipped you to interpret and *make relevant* difficult theological ideas to the people in the pews in a way that strengthens their *head*-to-*heart* connections," Sophia said. "It's a matter of common courtesy not to speak over their heads."

* * * *

"So, when *would* it be appropriate to preach about this tractate?" Benjamin asked.

"Probably never at Mass," Sophia said. "The pulpit is the wrong channel for advanced, unfiltered theological discourse. You need to find another more appropriate venue. For example, you could use the tractate to develop a retreat or a workshop for your parishioners, allowing plenty of time for interaction, reflection, and prayer. Or you could choose an idea from the tractate and explain it in meaningful terms in your homily."

"It's beginning to sink in," Benjamin said. "You're really talking about respecting the people in the pews. Knowing that they want to grow in their faith—that they want to strengthen their *head*-to-*heart* connections. And helping them to encounter Christ in terms they can understand."

"Exactly," Sophia said. "Preaching at the intersection is about respect, not dumbing down. It's about meeting people where they are and using our gifts to mediate meaning. It's also about trusting that our parishioners will *want* to attend classes or workshops to learn more about our faith as they grow in their relationships with God."

PYLON FOUR: 'SPOKEN'

Scenario #3: Mismatched Messaging

"Next scenario, Benjamin: Can you remember a time when the preacher's verbal and nonverbal communication didn't 'match'?" Sophia pressed on.

"This one's easier," Benjamin said. "It was in preaching class. Naturally, we were all nervous. But a guy who was preaching on the Resurrection really stood out. He slumped over the pulpit and stared down at his written homily, somehow turning the joy of Christianity's definitive event into a dirge. He read to us in a slow, flat, monotonic voice. It was like he was seeing the words he'd written for the first time."

Sophia prodded, "And how did this experience make you feel?"

Benjamin's speech became more charged. "It's strange, but I felt *betrayed*. I felt: *if this guy doesn't have more conviction that this, why should I trust a thing he's saying*?!? I mean, after all, he was preaching about Jesus Christ—the greatest love story of all time!"

* * * *

Sophia sat quietly before asking, "What do you think was going on?"

Benjamin reflected, "I think his nerves got in the way. My classmate had done a great job writing his homily. His message was riveting *and* healing, and it spoke to the intersection. But instead of *proclaiming* the Good News, he was so paralyzed with fear that he *read* it to us without any semblance of confidence or conviction."

"You used two important words: 'proclaim' and 'read,'" Sophia observed. "How would you define the difference?"

Benjamin shrugged, "I know, but I'm not sure I can put it into words."

"I'll help," Sophia offered. "To *proclaim* is to say something important in a public, official, and definitive way. To *read*, by contrast, is to interpret written symbols for meaning. Preaching is about proclaiming, not reading."

* * * *

Benjamin puzzled, "Then why were we expected to write our sermons in preaching class? What was that all about? Don't you write something so it can be read? I mean, I must have written two-hundred pages worth of homilies in one preaching class alone!"

"Actually, writing your homily or sermon is one of the best ways to organize your ideas," Sophia explained. "It can help to ensure you have a strong introduction, since the people in the pews will tune you out if you don't quickly capture their attention. It can help you maintain cohesion and think through transitions. It can keep you focused and from standing at the pulpit and paraphrasing the readings the congregation just heard. And—as one great preacher who served as an Air National Guard chaplain so aptly put it—it can help you land the plane instead of circling the landing strip again and again.

"Many great preachers *do* write their entire sermons, and some even proclaim from them. The difference is in delivery—ensuring that *verbal* and *nonverbal* communication support each other and that you really *are* proclaiming," she stressed.

V.

"Certainly, we could consider many other communication scenarios," Sophia said, "but I am wondering if it's necessary? You know the principles, and you've proven you can apply them."

Benjamin exclaimed, "I've just realized something: The scenarios we've just run through have been healing exercises!"

"Please, say more," Sophia invited.

Benjamin continued, "You've challenged me to experience the new awareness of illness—preaching missteps that disrupt the spiritual wellbeing of a congregation. You've challenged me to name the illness, consider its cause, and—based on my

PYLON FOUR: 'SPOKEN'

understanding—make a judgment. You've also challenged me to internalize the remedy from the perspective of a person in the pews."

Sophia laughed, "Guilty as charged."

"But why these scenarios?" Benjamin asked.

"No special reason," Sophia replied. "We could just as easily have considered other violations of basic communication principles—things like Redundant Repetition, Repellant Religiosity, Ruthless Rambling, Pregnant... uh,... um... Pauses, and even what Dominican homiletician Honora Werner calls 'salad preaching' with an indigestible amount of 'Let us.' There are more ways to sabotage the Good News than there are letters in the alphabet. The list is endless. Your challenge is to be aware of the basic principles of communication, to practice them faithfully, and to exorcise violations whenever they cross your path."

* * * *

Benjamin sat quietly for several minutes before asking, "What else do I need to know?"

"One last thing: As you observed earlier, preachers *are* connecting the people in the pews to the greatest love story ever told. *Capture the passion!*" Sophia stressed. "Disciples of Christ homiletician and spiritual director Kay Northcutt makes this point brilliantly in her book, *Kindling Desire for God: Preaching as Spiritual Direction*:

"Northcutt recalls reading to renowned theologian Joseph Sittler, who had lost his eyesight as a complication of old age, when she was a student at the University of Chicago Divinity School. Between poems by Emily Dickinson, she asked him what effective preaching meant. She recalls that Sittler, who had been deeply relaxed, sat up and 'practically shouted':

> 'You preachers must be as vehement as hell about the perfectly obvious! Remember when Jesus came to Lazarus, and wept? How the crowd remarked, amazed, "See how he loved him!" Take that amazement—that

passionate love of God—into your pulpit. *That's* how effective preaching works. The church—*your* church—will be astonished."[1]

"It's this passion—this love that never dies—that is the remedy for every illness in the world. It's this passion—this love—that attracts people to a relationship with God and strengthens the *head*-to-*heart* connection. It's this passion—this love—that sets the world on fire. It's this passion—this love—that is the foundation of preaching that heals," she finished.

Sitting on the bridge in the purple- and pink-streaked dusk, Benjamin pondered Sophia's words and the mystical week. Finally, he spoke with the confidence and energy of graced love: "You know, I think I *can* take it from here."

"I know you can," Sophia replied. "The *spoken* pylon. Where the rubber meets the road. Where you *will* heal, Benjamin. *Even by your preaching.*"

---

1. Kay L. Northcutt, *Kindling Desire for God: Preaching as Spiritual Direction*, 9–10.

— Interlude —

Reflection on Wellbeing

Benjamin remained on the bridge, watching the purple-pink streaks fade into the deepest indigo sky. Far away from heavy air and city lights, bright galaxies echoed the story of creation long ago. Night-life sounds and smells of receding fresh-baked heat heralded the gentle awakening of a nocturnal world while tempered coolness enveloped him in a hug of grace.

What most mesmerized Benjamin was the idea that he'd not only embraced a spirituality of preaching that heals in the past week, but he'd experienced healing himself.

It had been a mountain-top week, a revelatory experience. But now, it was time to go home. For the first time in a long time, Benjamin realized he was at peace.

— Chapter 9 —

Retrospective

As Benjamin entered the classroom, his thoughts flashed back to the most mystical week of his life several years ago, the week he became a preacher.

He remembered fleeing to his family's tree farm to grapple with the conviction that God did not want him to preach and the painful events that had led to this conviction: The series of fragmented and seemingly-unrelated tasks that crowded every second of his ordained life. A sense of deepening alienation between him and his parishioners and him and God. The dark scowl of a parishioner during one particularly excruciating homily that had sent his spirit spiraling on a downward trajectory.

Benjamin had prayed for resolution. His prayers had been answered with four lessons that were permanently etched on his soul:

First, preaching is not just what we do to prepare and deliver a homily or sermon. It is who we choose to become in response to grace. It is a conscious, overarching, and intentional spirituality that we give voice to with every word and deed.

Second, Christian preaching is addressed to human beings who are created in God's image and likeness. Unlike the rest of creation, the human is endowed with the ability to contemplate what is happening and, through the language of word and deed, initiate healing in response to illness. The "anatomy" for healing is the triple-composite human anthropology: The Organism interacts with the world through the five senses. The Psyche fuels the human throughout life and is the seat of memory, imagination, fantasies, dreams, and emotions. And the Spirit (which is the same thing as consciousness) is the seat of thinking and choosing. Emotions serve as a type of Emergency Alert System that signal the loss of wellbeing—illness. An understanding of this anthropology gives the preacher invaluable insight about illness and healing.

Third, the aim of all Christian preaching should be to bring God's healing love to a wounded and suffering world. Christian healing addresses avoidable illness, the loss of wellbeing caused by disordered human desires. It seeks to reorient the human, who has placed undue emphasis on possessions, power, position, and prestige, to God. A metaphor for healing is building a bridge that connects the *head* (the human spirit with its capacity to think and choose) to the *heart* (God Who Is Love).

And fourth, there are four characteristics (or pylons) of Christian preaching that heals: Pylon One: It is centered on the Gospel, the Good News of Jesus Christ, who is the perfect expression of God Who Is Love. Pylon Two: It is *I*ntentional, flowing from a spirituality (life orientation) to preaching that heals. Pylon Three: It is *H*olographic, recognizing the interrelatedness of all creation and from that, the idea that the illness of one affects all. Pylon Four: It is *S*poken (or expressed), both verbally and nonverbally. Together, the first letter of each pylon form an acrostic: G/IHS, with G representing Gospel and IHS the first three letters of the Greek name of Jesus.

Turning to face his preaching class, Benjamin planned to elaborate on each of these lessons and on each pylon *before* asking his sudents to prepare one word of preaching. Through the gift of Sophia—Wisdom, he had learned that these lessons, once mastered, would make all the difference in the world.

And so, looking at the sea of worried faces before him, he smiled and gently asked, "What is preaching?," knowing that all would be well.

Bibliography

Boff, Leonardo. *Francis of Rome and Francis of Assisi: A New Springtime for the Church*. Maryknoll, NY: Orbis, 2014.
Brueggemann, Walter, et al. *Exilic Preaching: Testimony for Christian Exiles in an Increasingly Hostile Culture*. Edited by Erskine Clarke. Harrisburg, PA: Trinity, 1998.
Cannato, Judy. *Radical Amazement: Contemplative Lessons from Black Holes, Supernovas, and Other Wonders of the Universe*. Notre Dame, IN: Sorin, 2006.
Clinebell, Howard. *Basic Types of Pastoral Care and Counseling: Resources for the Ministry of Healing and Growth*. Revised and updated by Bridget Clare McKeever. Nashville, TN: Abingdon, 2011.
Davies, Stevan L. *Jesus the Healer: Possession, Trance, and the Origins of Christianity*. New York: Continuum, 1995.
Delio, Ilia. *Making All Things New: Catholicity, Cosmology, Consciousness*. Maryknoll, NY: Orbis, 2015.
Dossey, Larry. *Healing Words: The Power of Prayer and the Practice of Medicine*. New York: HarperCollins, 1993.
———. *Reinventing Medicine: Beyond Mind-Body To a New Era of Healing*. New York: HarperCollins, 1999.
Edwards, Denis. *Jesus and the Cosmos*. Eugene, OR: Wipf and Stock, 1991.
Ferngren, Gary B. *Medicine and Religion: A Historical Introduction*. Baltimore, MD: Johns Hopkins University Press, 2014.
Francis. *Evangelii Gaudium: The Joy of the Gospel [Apostolic Exhortation on the Proclamation of the Gospel in Today's World]*. Frederick, MD: Word Among Us Press, 2013.
———. *Laudato Si: On Care for Our Common Home* (Encyclical Letter). Frederick, MD: Word Among Us Press, 2015.
Goodall, Jane. *In the Shadow of Man*. 1971. Reprint, Boston: Mariner, 2010.
Goergen, Donald. *Teilhard de Chardin's Cosmic Christology and Christian Cosmology*. Chevy Chase, MD: Now You Know Media, 2014.

Grogan, Brian. "The Ignatian Way #2: Ignatian Spirituality: An Overview." http://www.ignatianspirituality.com/what-is-ignatian-spirituality/the-ignatian-way/the-ignatian-way-2-ignatian-spirituality-an-overview/.

Harris, Daniel E. *We Speak the Word of the Lord: A Practical Plan for More Effective Preaching*. Eugene, OR: Wipf & Stock, 2001.

Heille, Gregory. *The Preaching of Pope Francis: Missionary Discipleship and the Ministry of the Word*. Collegeville, MN: Liturgical, 2015.

Hilkert, Mary Catherine. *Naming Grace: Preaching and the Sacramental Imagination*. New York: Continuum, 2006.

Helminiak, Daniel A. *Religion and the Human Sciences: an Approach via Spirituality*. New York: State University of New York Press, 1998.

Ivereigh, Austen. "Pope Francis Takes Fresh Approach to Papacy." *OSV Newsweekly*, March 20, 2013. https://www.osv.com/OSVNewsweekly/Story/TabId/2672/ArtMID/13567/ArticleID/7879/Pope-Francis-takes-fresh-approach-to-papacy.aspx.

Johnson, Luke Timothy. *The Gospel of Luke*. Edited by Daniel J. Harrington. Sacra Pagina 3. Collegeville, MN: Liturgical, 1991.

Jones, Robert P., and Daniel Cox. "'The Francis Effect?" U.S. Catholic Attitudes of Pope Francis, the Catholic Church, and American Politics." Aug. 25, 2015. https://www.prri.org/wp-content/uploads/2015/08/PRRI-RNS-2015-Survey.pdf.

Kelsey, Morton. *Healing and Christianity*. New York: Harper & Row, 1973.

Kim, Yung Suk. *A Transformative Reading of the Bible: Explorations of Holistic Human Transformation*. Eugene, OR: Cascade, 2013.

———. *Resurrecting Jesus: The Renewal of New Testament Theology*. Eugene, OR: Cascade, 2015.

Küng, Hans. *Can We Save the Catholic Church? We Can Save the Catholic Church!* London: Collins, 2013.

Levine, Amy-Jill. *The Misunderstood Jew: The Church and the Scandal of the Jewish Jesus*. New York: HarperOne, 2006.

Lonergan, Bernard J. F. *Insight: A Study of Human Understanding*. San Francisco: Harper & Row, 1978.

Malina, Bruce and Richard L. Rohrbaugh. *Social Science Commentary on the Gospel of John*. Minneapolis, MN: Augsburg Fortress, 1998.

———. *Social Science Commentary on the Synoptic Gospels*. Minneapolis, MN: Augsburg Fortress, 2003.

Mallam, Sally. "The Human Journey: Introduction to Axial Age Thought." https://humanjourney.us/ideas-that-shaped-our-modern-world-section/axial-age-thought-spiritual-foundations-of-today/.

Mannion, Gerard. *Pope Francis: Preacher, Teacher, and Reformer*. Chevy Chase, MD: Now You Know Media, 2015.

Martin, James. *The Jesuit Guide to Almost Everything: A Spirituality for Real Life*. New York: HarperCollins, 2010.

Moloney, Francis J. *The Gospel of John*. Edited by Daniel J. Harrington. Sacra Pagina 4. Collegeville, MN: Liturgical, 2005.

BIBLIOGRAPHY

Northcutt, Kay. *Kindling Desire for God: Preaching as Spiritual Direction.* Minneapolis, MN: Augsburg Fortress, 2009.

O'Murchu, Diarmuid. *Inclusivity: A Gospel Mandate.* Maryknoll, New York: Orbis, 2015.

Pazdan, Mary Margaret. *Becoming God's Beloved in the Company of Friends: A Spirituality of the Fourth Gospel.* Eugene, OR: Cascade, 2007.

Pew Research Center. "Strong Catholic Identity at a Four-Decade Low in U.S." March 13, 2013. https://www.pewforum.org/2013/03/13/strong-catholic-identity-at-a-four-decade-low-in-us/.

Pilch, John J. *Healing in the New Testament: Insights from Medical and Mediterranean Anthropology.* Minneapolis, MN: Augsburg Fortress, 2000.

Reid, Barbara. *Taking Up the Cross: New Testament Interpretation through Latina and Feminist Eyes.* Minneapolis, MN: Augsburg Fortress, 2007.

———. *The Gospel of Luke.* Chevy Chase, MD: Now You Know Media, 2008.

———. *Wisdom's Feast: An Invitation to Feminist Interpretation of the Scriptures.* Grand Rapids, MI: Eerdmans, 2016.

Rubio, Sergio and Francesca Ambrogetti. *Pope Francis: His Life in His Own Words: Conversations with Jorge Bergoglio.* New York: Penguin Group (USA), 2013.

Russell, Heidi Ann. *Quantum Shift: Theological and Pastoral Implications of Contemporary Developments in Science.* Collegeville, MN: Liturgical, 2015.

Schneiders, Sandra M. *The Revelatory Text: Interpreting the New Testament as Sacred Scripture.* 2nd ed. Collegeville, MN: Liturgical, 1999.

Spadaro, Antonio. *A Big Heart Open to God.* New York: America Press, 2013.

Spotts, Matt. "What's So Weird About a Jesuit Pope?" *The Jesuit Post*, March 14, 2013. https://thejesuitpost.org/2013/03/whats-so-weird-about-a-jesuit-pope/.

Swimme, Brian Thomas and Mary Evelyn Tucker. *Journey of the Universe.* New Haven, CT: Yale University Press, 2011.

Streeter, Carla Mae. *Foundations of Christian Spirituality: The Human and the Holy, A Systematic Approach.* Collegeville, MN: Liturgical, 2012.

———. "The Dominican Genius: Integrity and Balance." Lecture series presented in observance of the 800th anniversary of the Dominican Order, February 16—March 2, 2016. https://heartlandspirituality.teachable.com/courses/44905/lectures/783083.

———. *The Human and the Holy: Foundations of Spirituality.* Chevy Chase, MD: Now You Know Media, 2010.

Teilhard de Chardin, Pierre. *The Phenomenon of Man.* New York: Harper Perennial Modern Classics, 2008.

Teilhard de Chardin, Pierre, and Ursula King. *Writings.* Modern Spiritual Masters Series. Maryknoll, NY: Orbis, 1999.

Tilley, Terrence W. *The Disciples' Jesus: Christology as Connecting Practice.* New York: Maryknoll, 2008.

Tornielli, Andrea, and Giacomo Galeazzi. *This Economy Kills: Pope Francis on Capitalism and Social Justice.* Collegeville, MN: Liturgical, 2015.

United States Conference of Catholic Bishops. "Fulfilled in Your Hearing: The Homily in the Sunday Assembly." Washington, DC: USCCB, 1982. https://www.usccb.org/beliefs-and-teachings/vocations/priesthood/priestly-life-and-ministry/upload/fiyh.pdf.

Urion, David K. *Compassion as a Subversive Activity*. Cambridge: Cowley, 2006.

Vidal, John. "Global Warming Causes 300,000 Deaths a Year, Says Kofi Annan Thinktank." *The Guardian*, May 29, 2009. https://www.theguardian.com/environment/2009/may/29/1.

Wallace, James A., ed. *Preaching in the Sunday Assembly: A Pastoral Commentary on Fulfilled in Your Hearing*. Collegeville, MN: Liturgical, 2010.

www.ingramcontent.com/pod-product-compliance
Lightning Source LLC
Chambersburg PA
CBHW070500100426
42743CB00010B/1694